"In *ALL I[N]* ... ugh and tough enou[gh] ... [the] limit in terms of th[e] ... [look]ing for a kick in the p[ants] ... this is the book for you."
—**Katherine Wintsch**, Author of *Slay Like a Mother*, CEO & Founder of The Mom Complex

"*ALL IN* by Carrie Fabris is an unapologetic and honest account of the challenging balance of work-life and mom-life experienced by so many women today. Carrie's moving stories and insightful lessons will leave you reaching for a glass of wine, crying "PREACH" at the top of your lungs, and finally prioritizing the self-care that you deserve. If you are a mom, know a mom, or have a mom, you should buy this book."
—**Tracy Timm**, Author of *Unstoppable*, Founder of Thrivist

"*ALL IN* is a powerful, real and inspiring story that will make you laugh, cry, feel motivated, and want to take action to go claim your best life. Carrie holds nothing back as she shares her struggles and triumphs with a dynamic vulnerability. Not only working moms need this book, every mom needs this book to ensure they go all in on themselves."
—**Natalie Boyle**, CEO & Founder of Mommies In Need

"Carrie is the kind of girlfriend every adult woman should have: honest, raw, wise and full of heart and laugh out loud stories. What she has done with this book/memoir/self-help book is tear open her own heart and life to make sense of it, taking us along her journey towards self-love and self-actualization. Reading her chronicle, you come to realize that these struggles are more universal than we often realize they are, and then, Carrie shares real-world, practical tips on how to move forward. Since not everyone can have a Carrie Fabris for a friend or coach, this is the next best thing."
—**Kimberly A. Kho**, MD, MPH, Strauss Family Chair in Women's Health, UT Southwestern Medical Center

"The struggle of seeking fulfillment while juggling a demanding career and a family who needs you is one of the greatest challenges of our lifetimes. Mom guilt, anxiety, exhaustion. Repeat. *ALL IN* depicts a raw and real story that inspires us all to release our fears, embrace our passions, put ourselves first every now and then, and JUICE up our lives…unapologetically."
—**Kayla Brown**, Chief of Staff, Axios Media

"As a mother of two and a business owner, I read *ALL IN* after neglecting most of my personal needs for over a decade. Carrie's journey and tough love advice motivated me to take action and start my own journey to become a better mother and wife by becoming a better version of myself. Before I finished *ALL IN*, I was already developing new habits, setting more realistic goals and putting in place a support network to make it stick."
—**Deanna Centurion**, Founder & Chief Strategy Officer, Cyera Strategies

"We were never called to live apathetic or milk toast lives. Yet circumstances can cause us to settle for less than our greatest purpose. Carrie gives us a transparent, gritty behind-the-scenes look at the hard-earned experiences that have made her the widely recognized leader that she is today. Through, *ALL IN*, Carrie invites us to get unstuck, go 'all in', and take the quest to claim and seize that juicy life."
—**Taylor L. Cole**, APR, TV Host, Executive Producer, Faith-based Leader, Founder of TVwithTLC.com

"The working mom's life can be a walk – not in the park – but on a tightrope. Pumping while you PowerPoint becomes an Olympic win! But armed with this brilliantly humorous – and at times heart-breaking – book that Carrie Fabris has penned, you'll be astounded when you realize what a badass you really are. The fact that you even bought this book is a sign that you're ready…ready to live your best working-mom life!"
—**Susan C. Freeman**, Stevie® Award-winning CEO & Founder, Freeman Means Business, M.A., Ph.D. Scholar

"In *ALL IN*, Carrie Fabris is raw and authentic in describing her fight to live a life of her choosing and free of expectation. Her story is refreshing because it invites every one of us to ask ourselves: What life do I want?"
—**Emma Sharma**, Founder & Principal of Swallowtail Group, Board member, former C-suite Executive & General Counsel

ALL IN

A WORKING MOM'S UNAPOLOGETIC QUEST FOR A JUICY LIFE

CARRIE FABRIS

All In
Copyright © 2022 Carrie Fabris

First Edition

All rights reserved. No part of this publication may be reproduced, stored in, or introduced into a retrieval system, or transmitted in any form, or by any means (electronic, mechanical, photocopying, recording, or otherwise) without the prior written permission of the author, except in the case of brief quotations or sample images embedded in critical articles or reviews.

ISBN: 978-1-945587-77-1
Library of Congress Control Number: 2022905069

1. Self-help; 2. Career; 3. Women's Issues; 4. Motherhood; 5. Coaching.

Cover design: Alishba Shah
Typesetting and design: Dancing Moon Press

dancingmoonpress.com
Bend, Oregon
Lincoln City, Oregon

DANCING MOON PRESS

DEDICATION

For A.L.L. of my heart:

Andres, Lucas and Lala.

You are my why.

For my mom, Nancy. I miss you every day and feel your presence.

I love you to the edge of eternity and back.

Table of Contents

FOREWORD 9
INTRODUCTION: INVITATION TO A JUICIER YOU 15

PART 1: FRUSTRATED   19

CHAPTER 1: LONDON CALLING 21
Sipping Oxygen   21
Districting & Dollars   22
The First Sign & A Taste of Freedom   28
Wizarding World   30
The Second Sign   32
Find Your Juicy Life   35

CHAPTER 2: UNDER PRESSURE 37
CareerFrame   37
Home Sweet Home   39
Buy/Rent/Sell Hell   45
Anxiety Tipping Point   48
Desperately Seeking a Safety Net   51
Find Your Juicy Life   54

CHAPTER 3: THE BALANCING ACT 55
The Remark that Lit a Spark   55
Letting Go of "Just So"   59
It Takes a Village   61
Long Distance Two Stepping   62
Globe Trotting Groove Train   66
Find Your Juicy Life   68

CHAPTER 4: GRIEF WILL ROCK YOU 69

The Day the Music Died	69
The Show Must Go On	73
Intuition Strikes	75
Find Your Juicy Life	78
Lessons Learned through Frustration	80

PART 2: F.E.A.R.   83

CHAPTER 5: CRACKING OPEN 85

The Island, The Boat & The Rudder	85
Wave After Wave	89
Find Your Juicy Life	92

CHAPTER 6: THE UNEXPECTED GURU 93

Divine Timing	93
Unleashed	95
The Exorcism	99
Self-Love Over Logic	101
Find Your Juicy Life	104

CHAPTER 7: NAVIGATING REALITY 107

Infidelity	107
Mr. Mom Saves the Day	109
Dark Night of the Soul	112
Boot on the Ass	113
Find Your Juicy Life	115

CHAPTER 8: BREAKTHROUGH 117

Show Yourself	117
A Date with Destiny	119
The Pivotal Moment	122

The Warrior, The Magician and The Vault	124
Toward the Dream	127
Find Your Juicy Life	132
Lessons Learned through F.E.A.R.	134

PART 3: FULFILLED 137

CHAPTER 9: NO MATTER WHAT 139
Certifiable	139
Resigned Calmness	141
Damn Pandemic	143
Tears for Fears	145
Find Your Juicy Life	148

CHAPTER 10: TAKING CARE OF BUSINESS 149
Tweaking	149
The Sword of Pride	151
Obi-Wan	156
Find Your Juicy Life	158

CHAPTER 11: MASTERING 159
Solo Plunge	159
Check, Please!	162
Money Flows	163
The Soul Path	165
Find Your Juicy Life	169

CHAPTER 12: A JUICY LIFE 171
Captain Fantastic	172
Miss Glitter Sparkles	176
Pupper Nugget	181
Walking On Sunshine	183

Find Your Juicy Life	186
Lessons Learned through Fulfillment	188
CONCLUSION: PERMISSION TO BE UNAPOLOGETIC	**191**
AFTERWORD: A SALUTE TO MOMS WHO GO ALL IN	**195**
Purpose-Driven Nomad by Laura Helen	195
Showing Up Stronger by Danielle	198
Leaning In by Rian	201
Becoming Human by Amanda	203
Finding Balance by Andrea	205
Starting Over by Phoebe	207
Parting Words	209
ACKNOWLEDGEMENTS	**211**

FOREWORD

As a working mom of three children, I know first-hand what it's like to struggle with putting yourself first. I focused on the hustle and bustle of my kids when they were younger, all going in different directions, all while holding down a demanding full-time job. Through it all, I got left behind more times that I want to count, and the worst part was, I was the one that let it happen. Even as our kids grow, we still find ourselves putting everyone else's needs before our own. Fast forward to the present: my kids were all grown up and I found myself looking in the mirror, wondering for perhaps the first time: what did I want for me for the rest of my life? Something needed to change.

The first time I met Carrie Fabris in person was in July of 2019 on her front porch in Dallas, Texas at midnight with my heavy "baggage" slung across my shoulder. Flying in from Portland, Maine, I was weary. I had real baggage, my luggage, and huge, metaphorical, emotional baggage as my father had just passed away and I'd spent the last few months living away from home supporting my husband through cancer treatments. Sure, my kids were all grown up, but taking care of everyone else was a theme that had continued on. I was tired but I knew I wanted something more for myself than the grief that was consuming me. So I jumped on a plane to Texas to meet a woman I'd never met in person before.

I'd met Carrie during a yearlong online women's coaching program and was instantly drawn to her. She immediately stood out among the twenty or so rock-star women in our group. She was real, beautiful, motivated, sassy, a total badass with huge desires who was committed to getting things done that needed to get done. I found out that Carrie was going to attend a Tony Robbins event. I was not a fan of Tony Robbins at the time but what I was a fan of were Carrie's reasons for why she was going to attend this "life changing" event, and I wanted in. Watching Carrie through the various Zoom calls in our coaching program, she reinforced her strong desire for massive change and massive action. Even though I was a bit apprehensive of joining her for the Tony event, something about her determination was intoxicating. I trusted her, and so I took her lead and flew to Dallas, landing on her front porch that July night.

What I like most about my gorgeous dark-haired friend is that she is not afraid of getting messy. She is not scared of going deep to do the hard emotional work. She knows from experience that on the other side is pure joy and she truly wants this for others.

After our amazing Tony Robbins event, I got to know Carrie on a deeper, soul-sister level. How can you not after shedding millions of tears, deep belly laughs, panic attacks and walking on fire together? As a result of our fast friendship, Carrie was deeply vulnerable and I had a front row seat to her fear, shame, depleted money, lack mindset and dissatisfaction with significant parts of her life, namely her job and financial situation. I could relate to what it is like to be a kick-ass mom AND wife AND daughter AND sister AND friend all while trying to become the badass entrepreneur that you know is inside you. She was the epitome of frustrated—stuck and afraid to launch what she knew in her bones was her life's work. But what I could also feel were her passion and courage bubbling under the surface.

Don't get me wrong—this was not a seamless easy journey for my friend. It was raw and hard and quite exhausting to witness but it was also beautiful and inspiring. I witnessed Carrie battle through it all to find her freedom, her voice and her joy. Tony talked to us about juicing things up to make life livelier. At the time, I didn't realize how much that spoke to Carrie. From a distance, peppered with Zoom and phone calls, I watched and listened to her go from frustrated to fearful to fulfilled over the course of two years as she claimed her own juiced up life.

Throughout her journey, she was focused on reframing her mindset and knowing that she wanted to transform, thrive and live her version of her own authentic, fulfilled life. She also passionately wanted to influence and impact others to help elevate themselves personally and professionally, coaching them with her first-hand experience as a foundation for relatability.

I was so touched by her life story and resiliency that I knew in my bones she needed to share her journey. I had a feeling that others would heal and find ambition just by knowing that someone else had gone through similar hard things and managed to come out full of grace and grit. It is not every day that you get to witness someone go through such a powerful personal crisis to manifest a truly self-proclaimed compelling life. I went on repeat over a matter of months telling her to write her story. Thankfully for all of us, she finally listened.

Carrie is a natural coach and champion of women, and her story is a gift that continues to delight and influence me. I am so proud of her for sharing it with others. Her tough love, tell-us-what-we-need-to-hear, strengths-based approach to life and career is inspiring in many ways. She found her happy by unapologetically putting herself first.

When I was a working mom with kids still at home, I wish I would have had this book as a raw, real life, tell-it-like-it-is guide to help me feel human, to remind me of my own importance, to ensure me that my kids will not only be alive if I leave them in the care of someone else while I travel, they will also grow up to be amazing humans despite how many long hours they witnessed me work, and that I missed out on things from time to time.

The struggle with the juggle is real for working moms and Carrie doesn't pretend that it's easy. Instead, in this book, she helps us all see that it is okay and damn right necessary to set boundaries with our kids, our partners, and our careers so we can take care of ourselves for five seconds, and not apologize for it, nor ask permission. She helps us see that in order to take care of everyone else, we must take care of ourselves first.

By reading Carrie's story, hopefully you will see some of yourself in her and find the strength to do the things in your life that you really want to do, and do them now. Dive deep into this spunky memoir of hers with your heart wide open. It is a true gift of sisterhood, desire and realism with a side of extra-spicy Texas kick ass inspiration that we all need today. Carrie is without a doubt unapologetic about her journey that took her to new heights beyond her imagination. May we all be so bold. From here, I'll let Carrie share with you how she did it and how you can too.

Jessica Perkins
Entrepreneur
Working mom
EQ-I Certified Coach
Portland, Maine

14 ALL IN

INTRODUCTION

INVITATION TO A JUICIER YOU

Have you seen that American Greetings commercial? The one where people are being interviewed for a job and once they hear the requirements for the role, they think the interviewer is literally crazy? It's for a Director of Operations role.

The job requires that the candidate has a wide range of mobility, the ability to stand for long hours at a time, the flexibility to bend over multiple times within an hour, and a high level of stamina. The candidate is expected to be available for work 135—unlimited hours per week, 365 days a year, with no days off, no breaks, and no lunch, unless the associates have finished their lunches first. Weekends, weeknights, and holidays expected, especially on the associate's birthdays, Thanksgiving, Christmas, New Year's, Easter, and the entire summer when the workload will increase exponentially. The person must have excellent negotiation and interpersonal skills, be able to wear multiple hats, and have an unrelenting desire to give associates constant attention while working in chaotic environments.

The position requires an ongoing happy attitude with the understanding that the emotional connections created on the job are immeasurable. A degree in medicine, finance, and/or the culinary arts preferred. The salary is zero. Over two billion people hold this position, and if you're reading this book, you likely are one of them.

Being a mom is rewarding and joyful. It's also thankless and exhausting at times. Throw a career in the mix just for fun and the struggle with the juggle is real. As we go about taking care of our families, our businesses, our clients, and pretty much everyone around us, when do we get taken care of? Who is focusing on us? And if we keep waiting to be taken care of, how long will we have to wait?

Maybe the better question is: Why aren't we choosing to be our own heroes and focusing on ourselves? What if we decided to put ourselves first, for once, in order to more fully show up as moms, hold down careers that we love, and nurture our families all while nurturing ourselves? The cool thing is that we can make that decision! This book will show you how an ordinary mom (me) demanded a more fulfilled life and unapologetically went all in on herself to claim it.

This is my story. It's a snapshot in time where I chose to navigate hard personal challenges while momming hard, working full-time, and trying to keep my shit together, which often felt almost impossible without some escape mechanism often found in a bottle of wine or a bar of chocolate. I went from frustrated, fear-driven uncertainty to clarity and fulfillment. I learned some of life's most valuable lessons by allowing pain to be my teacher and courage to be my guide. Every step of the way, intention was with me.

For decades, I carried a heavy load of grief, insecurities, self-criticism, shame, and fear. It was not until I was 42 years old that I realized I could *choose* the life that lay ahead of me, regardless of my past. What I wanted was within reach, but only I could stretch and grow to reach it. I had to get so low, so full of anxiety, and to such a level of frustration that choosing to stretch was the only option. Through hard emotional, mental, and spiritual work, I was able to transform into someone full of energy, playing to my strengths, and claiming my power—also known as living a juicy life.

As you walk through the intimate details of the journey that took me from drama to nirvana, I will share some of the lessons I learned along the way. Working with coaches, attending seminars, shedding a lot of tears, and healing allowed me to finally find joy, which was patiently waiting to be embraced. I also share some suggestions of how you can juice up your own life by unapologetically putting yourself first. After all, your story and how you navigate it is up to you.

I often wonder what my life would look like today if I hadn't made the choice to go all in on myself. The five-year period of my life, represented in these pages, began in a place of worry, fear, and shame. I'm not necessarily proud of who I was back then, and yet, I realize that the only way I could find who I was meant to become was to face who I was. A specific challenge with my son ignited my journey but not everyone needs a trigger to make a choice for themselves. Every moment is the right moment to start, no matter what is happening around you. My hope is that by reading about my path to fulfillment, you will know that you are not alone and you will be inspired to strike out on your own path. The cool part about putting yourself first, all mom guilt aside, is that you will start to see change in yourself, and more importantly, so will everyone else around you.

Choosing to understand the pain from your past in order to unlock your future, getting unstuck, and giving yourself permission to juice things up is one hell of an awesome mid-life gift, not crisis. If you're a working mom, believe me, I know how busy you are, and I'm honored that you picked up this book. It means that something inside of you is curious about how to live your best, working-mom life. I want this for all moms out there who are taking care of everyone but themselves. It's your turn. Your family may not be able to verbalize it, but I promise you, they are counting on you to be your best. Unapologetically claim a juicy life for yourself, and for them. It's a win-win, and it's time to go all in.

PART 1
FRUSTRATED

CHAPTER 1

LONDON CALLING

> "It is our choices, Harry, that show what we truly are, far more than our abilities."
> —*Albus Dumbeldore,*
> *Headmaster at Hogwarts School of Witchcraft and Wizardry*

Sipping Oxygen

> *"Ladies and gentlemen, I'd like to direct your attention to the television monitors. We will be showing our safety demonstration for our flight today."*

Sitting in seat 2B, sipping pre-flight champagne, I tuned out the flight attendant's message like I often do (ok, always do). After a 20-year career in the travel industry, the safety announcements had long since faded to background noise. On this particular day, I was on an American Airlines 777 departing Dallas/Ft Worth headed to London for a vacation—blissfully alone.

It was November 2016, and I had two big decisions to make. Booking a trip to the United Kingdom—without my amazing husband Andres and two adorable children, Lucas and Lala—was the first step to giving myself the space and time to figure those decisions out.

> *"...In the event of a loss in air pressure, an oxygen mask will automatically drop from the overhead compartment. To start the flow of oxygen, pull the mask towards you. Place it firmly over your nose and mouth, secure the elastic band behind your head, and breathe normally. Although the bag will not inflate, oxygen is flowing to the mask. If you are travelling with a child or someone who requires assistance, secure your own mask first before assisting others."*

The champagne glass froze in my hand, pre-sip. Holy shit. I'd heard the safety instruction speech a thousand times before but this was the first time I actually *listened*. It was like the flight attendant, with her perfect British accent, was speaking directly to me alone. "Hello darling! You there, in seat 2B. Put your mask on first! Do you hear me? If you don't, you will wither up and die from exhaustion!"

Slowly sipping my champagne, I smiled and thought, "Yes, I hear you! And that's exactly what I plan to do for the next seven days." I savored the celebratory bubbles and the mental image of myself roaming the streets of London, free from the sweet, little demanding voices at home. The plan was to clear my head and do a lot of soul searching. I was going to look for clarity, and pay attention to the signs, and get in touch with my intuition.

"Hello darling! You there, in seat 2B. Put your mask on first! Do you hear me?"

Districting & Dollars

As the plane took off for London, I sat briefly with the two big decisions on deck. One of them had to do with Lucas, and the other one had to do with me. Separating them was not as straightforward as securing my own oxygen mask before assisting my child, who happened to need assistance.

Earlier in the year, I had become increasingly frustrated with Lucas' school. It was a precious private school for children with learning differences. Our son was diagnosed with learning differences when he was 4 years old and, whereas he had his challenges, behavior issues was not one of them. Yet, Andres and I started receiving notice after notice about his disruptive behavior in class. Apparently, Lucas was kicking kids under the table and had to be removed to the Director's office for a "time out"—on a practically daily basis.

I'm a mom who almost always sides with the teacher first. I will not have my children act like assholes in class. But kicking kids daily didn't sound like Lucas. I wanted to understand the real issue, which was when I realized how genius my son is and why this had become a consistent occurrence.

After some digging, the following chain of events came to light: Lucas kicks a kid, the kid cries out, the teacher sends Lucas to the Director's office. The Director's receptionist (who adores him) gives Lucas a big hug and chats him up. The Director's dog comes trotting out of the office, wagging her tail to play and be petted. Sending him to the office only reinforced my son's behavior issues because it was a great way to get out of class and schoolwork, while also getting to visit the receptionist and the dog. A brilliant strategy!

While I had to chuckle at my son's creativity, I was not happy that the teacher clearly did not see the bigger problem. Needless to say, this was not going to work for me. My kid is no perfect angel but he didn't have behavior issues either. I'm pretty sure he was bored out of his mind and doing anything he could to escape, in addition to simply not wanting to try at schoolwork. The combination of my growing frustration with how the school year had gone, or not gone, for my son and now this compounding "behavior issue" did not sit right, at all. Maybe it was time to move on to an environment that would help Lucas progress in the right direction.

I sought counsel from the psychologist who had diagnosed Lucas a few years earlier. (I trust her completely and adore her to this day.) She strongly suggested a different school district that offered what was called a Structure Program. She said it would be, "Perfect for Lucas. It's made for a kiddo just like him!" There was just one tiny little problem: we would have to move.

At the time, we lived in a darling neighborhood with an educationally inconsistent public school district. As such, Lucas and Lala went to private schools. The district the psychologist recommended, Park Cities, was among the best public schools in Dallas. It was also, unsurprisingly, the most expensive neighborhood in the city. Getting Lucas into the Structure Program translated to selling the house Andres and I had lived in for 10 years and finding a new house (in one of the most expensive neighborhoods), and we only had six months to do it.

In the face of all this, I started crying—not at the prospect of what was required, but at the prospect of the talk Andres and I needed to have. I worried he'd miss the whole point, and think this was me conspiring to move to a nicer house (where I'd have my own closet)! I told the psychologist, "I'm going to need a prescription from you for this new school district, and the move that's required as a result." That would help my talk with my husband, who has been known to be both analytical and skeptical.

As much as I didn't love the idea of bringing the move up, I also knew that when Andres and I came together, we could make anything happen, especially when it was important and involved our kids. This time, we needed to come together with our incomes, which I was not overly contributing to at the moment, to afford a house and enable Lucas to attend one of two specific elementary schools that offered the Structure Program. After presenting properly sourced data along with a couple of margaritas, of course, Andres was on board with the plan, and in order to execute, I had to activate on a few things.

I flew into action, set up tours of both schools, and arranged meetings with the principals and special ed teachers. Both schools looked great but we had a strong preference for Jeremy Gilbert, who is one of the most amazing principals I have ever encountered, to this day. His style was so personable. When we met with him, Andres and I both felt like he was talking to us as if we were the only parents in the world. He was enthusiastically curious about Lucas and had an energy about him that put us at ease while also getting us excited about moving to the district. He knew the names of every kid that walked into the office during our visit, and their parents too. He took a personal interest in every human involved with his school, and I wanted Lucas and our family to be a part of it all. All that was left to work through was bringing this plan to fruition, which meant funding it.

The truth is, our financial security was on shaky ground. Andres launched a start-up in 2008 and I had been the sole breadwinner for almost six years. Once he got Series A funding in 2013 and a steady salary, I was tired of the work, the business travel, and the stress of it all. I wanted to spend time with my babies who were then 1 and 3. It was a bittersweet decision to leave corporate after working for 20-plus years in travel for Travelocity, Google and most recently, Sabre. Yet, I was ready to hand the breadwinner baton over to my husband and soak up the adorableness of little Lucas and Lala.

The first two months of being at home was delightful. Two more months in, the delight started to fade as the realities of full time momming sank in. Two more months later, I found myself looking in the mirror, disheveled, missing adult interaction, and wondering what the hell I was doing. As much as I adore my children, I realized—after only six months—I was actually a happier mom when I had a career and could have intelligent conversations with other professionals. At Sabre, I led a team of 25 people who sought my counsel. At home, I was managing two tiny humans who didn't listen to a word I said.

At Sabre, I led a team of 25 people who sought my counsel. At home, I was managing two tiny humans who didn't listen to a word I said.

One day, while pushing Lala on the backyard swing, I looked up to the sky and thought, "Hey sky, if I could do anything I wanted, what would it be?" The answer was incredibly, and immediately, clear. I wanted to guide and support others at work. I loved leadership, I thought I was actually good at it, and I missed it. I wanted to do something that got me back to connecting with professional adults and allowed me to use my corporate experience, but that did not take me back into a corporate role working for "the man."

I decided to hang my freak flag and proclaimed myself "a career coach and leadership consultant." I'd never personally worked with a coach and, to be totally honest, I had no idea what was involved with being a coach. All I knew was that I was good at leadership. I had built and led loyal, high-producing teams, and I knew a thing or two about how to successfully navigate through organizations and make the right moves for growth. With my "say like it is" style, I could help others hear what they needed to hear and get where they wanted to go by making necessary tweaks and behavior changes. On top of it all, whenever I had been in a leadership role and a direct report told me that I helped them, it felt really good. My ego loved it, and my heart loved it even more.

From that point forward, whenever people asked that predictable, first, get-to-know-you question—"what do you do?"—I rattled off my new self-proclaimed title with total confidence and acted as if it were the most natural thing in the world. I had pretty much zero clue what it meant to be a consultant, yet the more I introduced myself this way, the more I started to get clients here and there.

A few months later, I was in Brooklyn visiting one of my best friends, Karina, and talking about how I wanted to help people reframe their careers. After a little brainstorm on her couch, my new business name CareerFrame LLC was born. Through CareerFrame, the plan was to help primarily women build their confidence at work and coach them towards achieving their career goals and dreams. I had acquainted myself with Gallup's CliftonStrengths® and started teaching myself about the personality assessment and its 34 talent themes. I would use the assessment as the foundation for anyone I coached so we could play to their natural strengths and help them succeed at work and in life. My personal goal was to have a flexible work schedule so I could put my kids first. By choosing this consulting path, I was on my way to having the right balance of kids and work.

Despite how much I liked the sound of what I did and the intention behind it, I was piddling (at best) with the business. Faced with moving to Park Cities for the new school district also meant facing the truth. What I earned working with my four to five clients, who at the time paid $85/hour for six hours, wasn't going to cover many, if any, of the bills. My income certainly wasn't going to make up the difference for a new mortgage at two and a half times the cost of the home we'd lived in for 10 years. I had some serious soul searching to do when it came to how I was going to contribute to our family income and which school would be best suited for Lucas.

But first, I was going to take full advantage of my First-Class experience on the flight to London with these two decisions at the front of my mind. For the next 10 hours, I drank every varietal of wine on the menu, ate every meal and morsel offered, and watched movies in my luxurious reclining pod until I fell asleep.

Before drifting off, I had a little chuckle recalling Andres' reaction when he learned I'd given myself a full upgrade for this momentous trip. Andres is an incredible human being and husband; he's also very analytical. I am not. He puts practically everything into an Excel spreadsheet or Venn diagram when assessing, strategizing, and evaluating options. I simply GO. When I booked a First-Class ticket (with miles from using my Citibank AAdvantage Premium Select MasterCard like a champ, plus hundreds of thousands of Advantage miles accumulated from years of business travel), he challenged me. He did a whole mile-by-mile cost comparison and was adamant that I fly coach round trip to save the miles for future travel.

I looked at him lovingly and said, "Oh, oops! Looks like I just booked Flagship First Class using miles that, again, I traveled to acquire!" Mind you, I didn't respond this way to purposely annoy Andres, or to be a bitch, or to be insensitive to the financial pressure we faced. I responded this way because the trip had nothing to do with him. It was for me to step away, gain mental clarity, and take a break. I was putting on my own oxygen mask first; I wanted to do it without anyone else's opinions, rules, "should-haves", or the like; and I was going all in.

Andres didn't have to like it, but I was not going to ask for his permission this time. I was in pursuit of time alone, and I needed to get my head around the whats, whys and hows of the decisions on our plates, to which my contribution would need to be a major part. And if the London Eye caught me crying into the River Thames in the process of sorting things out, so be it.

After a decent night's sleep in my First-Class pod, I woke up on the descent into Heathrow. With my (metaphorical) oxygen mask secured, I felt a giddy excitement for a completely unscheduled, do whatever-the-fuck-I-want-to-do week ahead.

The First Sign & A Taste of Freedom

Prior to boarding my London-bound flight at DFW airport, I stopped into the Admirals Club, which I had access to because of my flight status. It was full of men sitting alone at small tables. Spotting an empty two top, I set my stuff down, and made a beeline for a cart stacked with cheese, crackers and wine.

On the way back to my table, a man smiled at me with his arms outstretched signifying the silent "Hello! What are YOU doing here?" It was my former boss David from Sabre, the company I left to focus on being a full-time mom. My immediate thought was, "Interesting. Here I am heading off to figure out what to do about my career—go back to corporate or get serious about consulting—and here is my former corporate boss."

We embraced in a big hug and, as the universe would have it, he too was headed to London on my flight. He was going for World Travel Mart, one of the largest global travel conferences, which I had attended many times in the past. Because it had been literally years, the timing was not even remotely on my radar. It was highly likely that many people I knew from the industry would be hopping around London for the conference while I was there to do some soul searching. What an interesting coincidence.

Another former co-worker was on the same flight, so when we arrived at Heathrow, the three of us hopped the train to Paddington Station and caught up. David invited me to a big party Sabre was hosting that night, and I gladly accepted. Was this one of the signs I had asked for? Was the universe telling me to be open about going back to corporate? While it was wonderful to catch up with old colleagues at the party, I decided to give myself the full week to see what other signs might be thrown my way. Focusing on the work decision was not the first thing I wanted to do!

I'd been to London many times before but never alone. A friend of mine had a guest flat and graciously offered it to me complimentary for the week. I took her out to dinner and brought some of her favorite snacks over from the States, but it was not nearly enough of a thank you for her generosity. She gave me way more than a place to stay; she gave me the freedom and convenience to explore the city with fresh eyes, plus saving me the expense of a hotel for the week.

In the morning, I woke up in my friend's cozy flat (alone!), made coffee and an English breakfast with ingredients from the local market down the street, and asked myself: What do I want to do today? That's right… what did *I* want to do? With no one else's opinions to weigh or practicalities to consider, I thought: How lovely! And then went about planning my day.

My first stop was the Tower of London. I'd been there many times before but again, never alone. Nursing a massive hangover from the Sabre party, I slowly explored every nook and cranny of the fortress. I strolled by the spot where Anne Boleyn lost her head, admired the crown jewels on display, and studied Henry VIII's suits of armor from when he was skinny to later, when he was a fat, arrogant bastard. I was in a historic paradise with nowhere to be and zero pressure to rush through.

The days that followed took me to various beautiful parks and classic British pubs around the city. I had champagne at Harrods, bought Christmas ornaments at Liberty of London, and went out to Windsor to see the Queen's palace away from the palace. As a huge fan of *The Crown* on Netflix, which had just come out, it was fun to have a better understanding of the stories behind the gigantic portraits on display throughout the great rooms. I worked my way over to St. George's Chapel. Sporting my Anne Boleyn t-shirt with her signature "B" pearl necklace, I wanted to find Henry's tomb and tell him to fuck off. Being in a holy place, I felt a bit guilty but as I looked down at his magnificent eternal resting place in the floor, as opposed to the extravagant and gaudy tomb he had designed and expected for himself, I thought, "Karma's a bitch. Looks like you got what you deserved." Clearly, I'm team Anne. The excursion to Windsor massaged my love for history and the Royals, and I soaked it all up like a sponge.

At one point during the day, Andres called to check in. He remarked, "Hey, you know, we haven't heard much from you these past few days," to which I enthusiastically responded, "I know! Isn't it great?" On every other previous trip, either with him or on business, I blew up the phone for updates on my babies. This was the first time I simply trusted that they would be healthy, happy, and alive upon my return. It was the first time

I let go of all control, which was hugely liberating (and highly necessary).

Wizarding World

My most anticipated adventure to what I imagined heaven on earth would be for me still lay ahead: Warner Bros. Studios and the Wizarding World of Harry Potter where all of the Harry Potter films were made. I've always loved magic and fantasy, and that little girl in me lives on in my love for Harry.

It was Wednesday, November 9, 2016. Before I took off for Hogwarts, I checked the news back home. We had a new president. I stared in silence at the screen and then shut my laptop thinking, "And so it is. On to the wonderful Wizarding World!"

Adorning my Death Eaters t-shirt, I took Ubers, tube trains, and buses to get to the town of Leavesden, outside of London, where the movies were filmed. Upon arrival, I marveled at the magical paradise, wandered the Great Hall, admired the props, hung out in Hagrid's hut, walked through the Night Bus and Hogwarts Express, drank Butter Beer, and of course, strolled down Diagon Alley. I was unquestionably the only 40-something mom there solo, acting like a bright-eyed 9-year-old!

My ringing phone jolted me out of my Harry Potter happy place and back to reality. It was Andres, who was planning to leave Dallas that night and join me in London the next morning for a long weekend. We had plans to spend time with a group of his close friends from grad school who lived there, and one of them was the best man in our wedding. His 40th birthday party was that weekend and nothing was going to keep Andres from missing the event. After several days of alone time, I was looking forward to seeing my husband, though I was slightly annoyed by the timing of his call.

He said, "I think I'm going to postpone my flight. We have a new president and I just want some time to check on things with the business. I'll regroup and catch a flight out to join you tomorrow night instead."

This was too much to wrap my head around. "Wait, what? Why? Actually, you know what? I need to call you back."

At that exact moment, I was standing in line among a sea of expectant children about to experience the highlight of the day. I was NOT going to let a phone call about a presidential change ruin this epic moment!

Giving my cloak a flare—magic wand in hand—I mounted a broom in front of a green screen. It was my turn to whoop and holler while I flew over the River Thames, looking for Death Eaters, and directing spells to knock them out of the sky. Despite my thematic Death Eaters t-shirt, I was on the good side of wizardry.

My day had been a total blast. Just before leaving the Wizarding World, I asked a complete stranger to count to three and snap a picture of me on my phone. She counted down, I jumped into the air, flashed a big smile, and hung on tight to my cart pretending to barrel through the portal at Platform 9 ¾. It was the best day. My 9-year-old self felt complete.

After the photo, I called my husband back to truly seek to understand his concerns and delay. We discussed the new plan: he would fly to London the next day and we would carry on with our weekend plans with friends. I was excited for him to join me and a wee bit more excited to have one more night to myself in a city that was quickly winning my heart.

On the tube leaving Leavesden, I reflected on how this incredible trip came about to begin with. It all started with a conversation centered on one of my husband's biggest passions. Andres is a major "burner," which is someone who attends the annual festival in the middle of the Nevada desert called Burning Man. The focus is on community, art, self-expression and self-reliance (and nudity, in some camps, so I'm told). Thousands of people from all over the world fly in for it, and my husband has gone every year for years. Before we were married, he went for four days. After we were married and started having kids, he'd go for eight days, and now, 11 days is his norm. Every year, I stayed behind with the kids. As the length of his attendance grew longer, I became a little resentful and spoke up about it.

"Why is it that you get to go to Burning Man for eight to 11 straight days every year and play pirate of the desert, while I stay here and manage the household and the kids solo? That's total bullshit. Maybe I'd like to go away and play for a week or so!"

To my unexpected surprise, Andres said, "Ok, well, go somewhere!"

I stared at him with an "are you serious?" face to which he replied, "If you want to go somewhere, go! Book it! BYE!" So that's what I did, and now, here I was, making memories I would never forget.

The Second Sign

Outside of needing to make a decision for myself about a career move that would bring an income of any significance, I took this trip to sort through what our plan would be to get Lucas into the right school environment. There was so much uncertainty hovering around the entire situation. I was looking for a sign and boy, did I get it.

After Andres arrived, we descended on a great London restaurant with friends to celebrate our best man's 40th. At one point in the evening, his wife grabbed me and said I must meet her friend who splits her time between Austin and London. My immediate thought was, "It must be nice to be her!"

She and I instantly struck up a conversation and discovered that we both had sons named Lucas and they both had learning differences. What were the odds? I went on to tell her about our situation, how we were strongly considering moving to a new neighborhood, and how we were currently assessing two new schools for Lucas.

This charming woman asked where we lived in Dallas, and I told her we lived in Briarwood but were considering moving to Park Cities. I said, "There are two great options for schools, but we're leaning towards one in particular because the principal seems absolutely amazing."

She said, "Dallas is a great city, so many good options. Actually, my brother-in-law is a principal at a school in Dallas."

I thought to myself, *surely not*, but for shits and giggles, asked, "Who is your brother-in-law?"

"Jeremy Gilbert."

My whole body had chills from head to toe. I could not believe this was happening. That I would meet this woman, in London, at some random restaurant, and that she would have a direct line to the person Andres and I loved instantly, and who was the gauge for which school to send Lucas to.

"OH. MY. GOD! Come with me!"

I picked my jaw up off the floor and dragged the woman towards Andres across the bar. Still breathless from the *holy shit! How is this possible?* moment, smiling hard, and practically yelling from disbelief, I said, "BABE! Ask her who her brother-in-law is! Ask her!" I was pointing and beaming and God knows what else.

He looked at my new friend curiously and said, "Who is your brother-in-law?"

When she said Jeremy Gilbert, Andres looked at me and said, "No fucking way!"

We started laughing. I said, "If THAT's not a sign, I don't know what is!"

Something had been telling me that Jeremy Gilbert was our metaphorical North Star for Lucas and here was the universe, winking at my instinct.

After checking the box for which direction was best for Lucas, I recalled how this whole trip had kicked off with an unexpected run-in with David from Sabre. I thought again about going back to corporate or building my consulting business, and decided to firmly plant one foot in each lane and see what happened. When I got home, I would hit the ground running towards securing a steady income to allow my family the opportunity to bring the plan for Lucas to fruition. If we needed to move to an expensive neighborhood, I would do whatever was necessary.

...here was the universe, winking at my instinct.

As Andres and I waited for our Uber to take us to Heathrow, I started to cry. I turned to look at him with tears streaming down my face and said, "I don't want to leave. Of course, I miss the babies but this trip, this time alone, this time to reflect and breathe has meant the world to me. Now I have clarity on a plan, and what I need to do to execute on that plan. This has truly been the best week of my adult life. Thank you for giving me the space to do this. It was exactly what I needed."

He hugged me tightly, wiped away my tears, and said, "You deserved it, Mama. Thank you for all that you do for the kids and me. You should definitely do this again."

Nestled in my seat for the flight home and ready for takeoff, the flight attendant yet again asked us to direct our attention to the safety video. This time, I listened to every word. When we were told to put our oxygen mask on first in the case of a loss in air pressure, I was prepared. After adorning my metaphorical oxygen mask and only assisting myself for a full week, my head was clear. Best decision. Ever.

Find Your Juicy Life

Book a solo trip.
Go somewhere alone for at least three days, ideally a week, and make it totally your decision. If this idea terrifies you, it is an indication of how badly you need to do it. Being alone can seem scary because we are left with our own thoughts, our own voice, and our own decisions. Yet, alone time can spark unimaginable growth. Let go and trust that the people caring for your children will keep them healthy, safe, happy and alive. Let go of the rigid routine and regimen and "let the world shape them," as my husband reminds me. More importantly, let it shape you and remind you of your potential. No one's permission is needed but your own.

Trust the signs.
Trust that the signs in front of you are telling you something. You are either on the right path or you need to pivot. Signs from the universe, or God, or whatever you believe in, are literally everywhere. Often, we are too busy to see them. When we slow down, and look, they start to pop up like arrows on a pre-destined path. Look for them, listen to them, seek to understand the connections, and then, stop trying to control everything. Allow things to simply unfold beautifully before your eyes.

CHAPTER 2

UNDER PRESSURE

> *"Cause love's such an old fashioned word, and love dares you to care for the people on the edge of the night, and love dares you to change our way of caring about ourselves."*
> *– David Bowie*

CareerFrame

After the trip to London, and with one foot in each lane job-wise—corporate track and consulting track—I started networking along each path. The more calls I made, the more I was reminded of the "working for the man" limitations I would have in corporate, and the more clarity I had on the career question. My heart was telling me to embrace my consulting business and help others reframe their careers. Promptly, I started on reframing *my own* career. For the next few months, I focused my networking on landing something, anything of some magnitude, as a consultant that would bring in legit income and allow us to afford a house in Park Cities.

By the New Year, the best of both worlds collided. I landed my first official corporate client for CareerFrame with a toy company in Dallas. The Chief HR Officer was someone I had cold-called via LinkedIn a year earlier. We had an instant connection over the phone, followed by one of the most fun coffee meetings I'd ever had, and a friendship ignited. She was one of the first people I called when I decided to focus on CareerFrame. Knowing about my foundational practice of using CliftonStrengths®, my HR friend brought me in to be the internal strengths coach and trainer and to support other HR needs as they arose. If you've ever watched the show *Billions* on Showtime, I was proclaimed the "Wendy Rhoades" of the toy company. I'll take that compliment any day!

The opportunity was perfect but it required some adjustments to get back into the full-time working-mom groove—if such a groove exists. The toy company wanted me in the office Mondays through Thursdays, with Fridays (blessedly) off. Since leaving Google, I had always worked from home, except when I was travelling. Those days, it was rare to do a video conference call. So no one cared or saw what I wore, which was usually workout clothes and a baseball hat. I was not used to getting up at 6 a.m. to shower, put on full make-up, do my hair, and select a professional outfit before waking up my kiddos, getting them ready for the day, driving them to two different schools, and heading into an office. At the end of the workday, we did the whole thing in reverse. And exercise? Forget it. I wanted sleep more that I wanted to sweat. This schedule will sound familiar to most working moms, but I was not nearly as accepting or gracious about it as they likely are.

> **It required some adjustments to get back into the full-time working-mom groove—if such a groove exists.**

With this new reality, I was unspeakably grateful for Fridays which became sacred time when I had an opportunity to relax, breathe, and reboot—something a lot of moms don't get nearly enough of. Every Friday, I took myself to what I called "Mama Lunch." I would pick a restaurant in the city, book a table, and just sit there people-watching, journaling, or reading, and always with a glass of wine.

After several months, I didn't love the Mondays through Thursdays routine, but I loved the toy company gig and was immensely grateful for it. (I loved it even more that they hired me with Fridays off.) The work itself juiced me up, and it felt unspeakably good to use my brain and interact with grownups.

Home Sweet Home

Still laser focused on getting Lucas to Jeremy Gilbert's school, Andres and I put our house on the market in the spring. Though we were committed to moving and excited about a new chapter, the house had a deep hold on our hearts. I found it in 2006 right before we got married. The second I walked in for the first time, I knew it was going to be our first home. It was a 4-bedroom, two-story "cottage" with Austin stone on the outside, vaulted ceilings, cream-colored walls, three fireplaces, a wine refrigerator, a stand-alone ice machine, and a gigantic Sub-Zero refrigerator to die for in a darling kitchen that overlooked the living room. To be honest, I wanted the house the instant I saw that refrigerator.

I called Andres and said, "Babe, I think I found our newlywed home. You have to come see it!" The next night, we went back to look at it together. As anticipated, he was sold on the refrigerator, too. Immediately after the viewing, we went out to dinner around the corner to calculate our offer. Within a week, the house was under contract, and we moved in three weeks before our wedding.

For the next 10 years, we grew our marriage and built our lives there. We had numerous dinner parties with friends and even had Princess Diana's former chef, Darren McGrady, cook eight of us dinner once. We loved every minute within those walls and all that we created and birthed inside of them.

The first year of our marriage in that house was full of stability, newlywed bliss and beyond-comfortable cash flow. Then, Andres enlightened me on a dream of his that had been brewing since grad school. He had written a white paper about a travel start-up and wanted to bring it to life. Andres is more of a risk taker than I am. He is often focused on tomorrow, while I'm sorting through today. After many discussions, he left his corporate job with Travelocity, with my full support, to launch his start-up out of the upstairs media room. I had a nice paying job at Google, so he could focus on building a business for our future while I would focus on paying for our lifestyle in the present. It was April 15, 2008, and the country was on the brink of a financial crisis.

On July 3, an executive from Google New York came to Dallas to announce they were closing the office. We were all given the option to relocate to another city or take a package. I took about 100 deep breaths and drove home to tell Andres the news. When we agreed he would take the leap from his nice paycheck to no paycheck, I told him, "Go for it, I've got this." When I got home that day, trying to hold it together, I said, "Babe, I don't got this!"

I decided to go for a jog to clear my head and process the news. Instead, my mind started to race, and the tears started to fall. (It's the only time in my life I've cried while jogging.) I was the sole breadwinner and now my cushy job was asking me to choose: relocate or take a package. If we relocated, we'd have to sell our new home and leave Dallas just as we were starting our married life there. If I took a package, I'd immediately have to start looking for another job. We'd only been in our house for a year, I adored it, I loved being close to my family, and at the time, I couldn't see beyond Dallas. My roots in Texas were deep. The more I cried, the more I realized what I wanted to do.

Back at the house, Andres was waiting and wondering what I'd come up with. I told him adamantly, "I don't want to move. I love this house, I love what we are building here, and I know it's Google, but I'll find another job. I'm taking the package, and we are going to make this work."

To Google's credit, they gave us a three-month lead to ensure we had enough time to relocate or find another job. I immediately started networking, and as the office closing date approached in October, I had two job offers in hand: one at Expedia and the other at a digital ad agency.

Neither salary came close to what I made at Google. Against my gut, I turned Expedia down and went to the agency, which offered $20K more. I was strictly following the money. By the third month, I'd been there long enough to have zero fit with the environment and feel beyond miserable. I started praying... "Dear layoff gods, please lay me off so I can get unemployment benefits and Cobra. Neither will come close to paying for the electricity bill or a doctor's appointment but at least it will be something. Amen." Two months later, the layoff gods answered my prayers. Hallelujah.

Andres continued to focus on getting his start-up off the ground while I went back to job searching. I landed a VP of Sales role at a small start-up travel company. The problem was, I could not understand what the hell the company was selling. The product was cumbersome; it was trying to compete with other more successful travel companies in its niche, and it was struggling. As investors started to get leery, and my team struggled to sell, the founder started asking for salary reductions. I was making the equivalent of what I'd been making six years prior and couldn't cover all of our basic expenses. Seven months into the job, as the company continued to suffer, I was let go—yet another financial blow.

My ego was taking a massive beating. I looked back over my career thus far and saw seven years at Travelocity, four years at Google, and now two layoffs back-to-back. I couldn't help but recognize that our combined household income had gone from something really nice to exactly $0 within a year of my leaving Google and Andres launching his business. Understandably, he did not want to give up before he got started, so I went back to networking.

My next best opportunity was back at Sabre, the parent company to Travelocity, where we'd both worked previously. I never thought my path would lead me back but here I was, beyond grateful for the stability and familiarity. The salary was not at Google's level, but it was better than the two hops I'd had recently.

While the financial turmoil unfolded, our mortgage, car payments, insurance, groceries, bills, and all of our living expenses were still due, and I couldn't keep up with it all on my salary alone. It was the beginning of a debt wave we would ride for years to come, dipping into our savings, selling stock, and driving up credit card balances to make ends meet.

The financial meltdown of 2008 left us badly bruised, emotionally and financially. Regardless, Andres and I leaned into each other and kept each other sane through the adversity, still loving our little home. We had pressures but we were not going to be frozen with fear, have zero fun, and wallow in our situation. More importantly, we wanted to expand our family and fill our precious home with the pitter-patter of little feet.

> *... we were not going to be frozen with fear, have zero fun, and wallow in our situation.*

Andres and I tried for 19 months to get pregnant with our first child. At about month 16, I was done with the emotional roller coaster and the planned sex. It sucked all the joy out of making a precious baby. By that point, we'd had every test run on us both. The awesomely frustrating part was that there was nothing wrong with either of us. We were damn near perfect, except I was not catching what Andres was shooting my way.

I could have saved us both a lot of heartache, waiting, and wondering if I knew then how mental stress impacts the adrenal system, which shuts down the reproductive system. It's nature's way of saying, "Hell no, I'm not letting anything get through and grow in that toxic environment!" My stress level had been off the charts for close to two years as the sole breadwinner while Andres built his start-up. My reproductive system let it be known that it was not open for business.

With the help of a fertility doctor, we made a plan. I got on 5 m.g. of Clomid, then increased to 10, and eventually brought in Follistim injections. I remember my alarm went off one night when I was meeting with a client in town from Las Vegas. Glass of wine in hand, I let him finish his sentence, quickly excused myself to the ladies room to give myself an injection, sashayed back to the table, picked up my wine glass, and carried on about business.

In September, we did IUI and attempted to make a baby holding hands with our doctor there for the party. If you've ever done fertility treatments, you know the extreme opposite of romance that surrounds it is almost comical. But when a beautiful baby, or two or three, is the result—who the fuck cares? Two weeks later, my boobs hurt and all I wanted was a pickle on a salt and vinegar chip. Bingo!

Nine months and 12 hours of labor later, followed by an emergency C-section, with the umbilical cord wrapped around his neck and torso like a Texas lasso, Lucas Harris entered the world on June 17, 2011 at 7:31 p.m. He was a big boy at 9 pounds, 3 ounces. He came into this world on a Friday (his favorite day of the week) with a delayed cry and eyes wide open.

Lucas was perfect. Andres and I bundled him up and took him home to all the sleepless wonder, joy, and middle of the night feedings a newborn brings. We all adjusted to our new little family life, and after my maternity leave, back to work I went to bring home the bacon, now for a family of three and even more to juggle emotionally and financially. Despite the adversity, I was madly in love with our baby boy and soaked up everything about him that I could. Things were going well at Sabre, and nice commission checks helped with our finances, though we were miles away from being out of the woods.

Given the difficulties we had getting pregnant the first time, and the fact that Andres and I were not getting any younger, we decided to start trying for baby #2 just before Lucas' first birthday. If we weren't successful "the ole fashioned way" after six months, we were prepared to give fertility treatments another go.

One Sunday afternoon, while Lucas was down for his nap, Andres and I decided to take a "nap" too. Two weeks later, I was pregnant. One and done. It was way too easy. I took three pregnancy tests before I could believe it was real. Weeks later, at a sonogram appointment, they announced, "You're having a girl!"

What? Wait! Me? I was a doe in the headlights staring at the ceiling, and thought, "Oh shit. What am I going to do with a girl?" I was terrified from pretty much the moment I learned we were having a daughter.

My own mother died three weeks after my 9th birthday from breast cancer. She was only 38; exactly the age I would be when my baby girl was born. Growing up without my mom, and now with a daughter of my own on the way, all I could think was, "What if I screw this up?" As a tomboy most of my younger years and raised by my dad, I understood boys and men more than girls. Boys were simple. Girls were drama. I felt ill equipped to handle girl stuff and was convinced I'd fail in some way.

I remember standing completely naked in the bathroom about to get in the shower. Looking at my huge belly in the mirror with a feeling of horror, I said to Andres, "This is going to be bad. By the time she starts her period, I'll be going through menopause! This is going to be really bad!" Andres just laughed and told me to stop pre-worrying.

On February 11, 2013, Lillian Grace was born at 8 pounds, 12 ounces at 7:59 a.m. on a Monday, her favorite day of the week. She came a week early, via a scheduled C-section. She came out screaming her head off as if demanding a blanket to shield her from the cold air attacking her body.

From the second they handed her to me, I fell hard in love—like I've never loved another human. Every fear, every worry instantly evaporated, and my heart doubled in size to create space for her. To this day, when I talk about the incredible human my daughter is and all she has taught me, I get teary-eyed. Within a year, Lucas nicknamed her "Lala" and it stuck.

Every fear, every worry instantly evaporated, and my heart doubled in size.

As the kids grew, their unique personalities and gifts started to emerge. It's beautifully funny how their journeys through life (so far) have been very similar to their individual paths to conception.

Lucas was slow to learn to walk at 16 months old, and seemed to be uncomfortable with any type of sensory overload. We noticed he had a speech delay, amongst other challenges and gifts. This took us on a journey of evaluations and therapists, and eventually to a diagnosis that led to the school where he was sent to the front office for behavior issues.

Lala presented a fresh steadiness amongst Lucas's topsy turvies with her magnetic positivity. An early overachiever, she started walking at 10 months, flashing her big brown eyes and smiles on the regular. Always curious, always singing, and always "easy," she got into every pre-school we applied to.

Both of my babies had their unique paths to entering life on this planet and have had their own path ever since then. And both are absolutely perfect in my eyes and teach me invaluable lessons every day.

For 10 years, our darling first house in Briarwood stood steady at the center. We had lived, entertained, loved, and brought our babies home there. Putting it on the market was heartwrenching. But once the decision was made, I was determined (and adamant) it was going to sell, and sell fast!

Buy/Rent/Sell Hell

If you've ever tried to sell a house with two small children, and a husband running a business out of it, you know it's a bitch. How does one keep everything perfectly staged and clean, and ensure no dirty hands touch the newly painted walls? While our realtor managed the actual showings, I tried to manage the scheduling of the showings. Every time I got a text with a showing request, I went into full OCD mode and became overly optimistic that THIS was our buyer. I spied on the people touring our house through our Ring doorbell. (Yes, I was that freak, and I still jump out of my skin whenever I hear the Ring doorbell chime on someone's phone.) Then, I'd wait—as patiently as someone sitting on a hot stove—to hear the outcome. It was never what I wanted to hear.

As months went by, the showings decreased and my anxiety increased. Without any offers, we still needed an address in Park Cities to get Lucas situated for the fall. Ever since Andres and I first discussed this scenario, I thought renting a house was likely the best path for us. It would give us a chance to ensure the new neighborhood and school were the right fit without having to buy and sell another house under pressure. It would also send a strong signal to Andres that this move was really not about me getting my own closet.

Still, we looked at all types of scenarios: houses for sale, condos for rent, we even put an offer on a home and got rejected because my sparse income did not satisfy the lenders. (Of course, they look at what you *made*, not what you are *currently making*. What's with that, by the way?)

We flapped our wings all over town while a perfect house sat available for rent in the heart of Jeremy Gilbert's school district. For months, I refused to even consider it a possibility. Why? Because it sat next door to a house I had spent countless hours in with a former close friend, who I call the Sales Badass. Our friendship had gone sour a year earlier, and I could not disassociate my family's immediate housing needs from my own ego bullshit, which was tied up in how the relationship ended. For the longest time, I wouldn't admit my reason for rejecting the house to anyone because I knew it was absurd, and the ridiculousness of it all was embarrassing.

When we first met, the Sales Badass and I had become fast, fierce friends. She earned the nickname because she was a sales machine. Sales was not something I enjoyed or was particularly good at; it was well out of my comfort zone. My sweet spot was account management and leadership. But she mesmerized me to the degree that I agreed to do business development for her part-time. At the peak of our personal and professional relationship, we spent a lot of time over at her house, strategizing and calling prospects, while she cheered me on.

The friendship was intense but it burned out as quickly as it flared up. I told myself it was because I didn't want to do sales. The truth is, we were at different places in our lives. I made some unfair judgments and assessments of hers while thinking pretty highly of my own. Focused on our differences versus all the fun and love we shared as dear friends, I told her I wanted to move on, make more money, do my own thing—anything to convince myself of my own importance. To her credit, she let me go and do whatever it was I thought I needed to go do. She let me think and feel what I needed to, and because of my behavior, we grew apart.

When I discovered the house next door to hers was for rent, she had already moved to another part of town. I wouldn't even have to worry about running into her. And yet, for *six months* (an unheard of amount of time for a rental house to remain available in Park Cities), I didn't even consider renting the house for the ridiculous reason that I didn't want to have to think about her every time I pulled in the driveway.

My twisted rationale had nothing to do with the Sales Badass and everything to do with me and my own bullshit. The humiliation I felt about the way things ended with her stood squarely between what I said I wanted for my family and what I was willing to do about it. Not one of my finer moments, that's for sure.

When I finally admitted, out loud, the utter absurdity of my thought process—and the fact that months had gone by and we still had nowhere to live in Park Cities—Andres and I went to look at the house. Despite my waffling, it had remained vacant, and seemed to be waiting for us.

Of course, it was perfect in size (if not too big), amenities and location. We signed the lease and took a deep sigh of relief that Lucas could enroll at his new school, under the leadership of Jeremy Gilbert. Goal achieved.

The relief was tempered, sadly, by a practical reality. Our house was still on the market. We had to carry our mortgage and pay for our new rental home while we sat in limbo waiting for a buyer to appear. Every passing day whispered lost money into my ear, and my anxiety thrived on it.

I was tired, highly stressed, and ready to move forward, so we decided to take half of our stuff to the new house and leave the other half behind for staging. At least we could get the kids settled into the new home while Andres and I waited for a nibble on our house.

Every passing day whispered lost money into my ear, and my anxiety thrived on it.

Despite the financial pressure, we had an extraordinary trip planned to San Miguel, Mexico to celebrate our friends' 10th wedding anniversary. It wasn't going to be just a few couples; about 60 other people from all over the country were flying in for the occasion. We couldn't conceive of missing out. Irresponsible, yes. Necessary to celebrate our dear friends, absolutely.

A few days before we were scheduled to leave, two things happened. The first thing was that we got an offer on the house. Eureka! We were elated and relieved until the deal fell apart. The buyer found mold at the inspection, which is a common and solvable issue in Texas, but being from Chicago, he wasn't having it. He dramatically dropped his offer to an insulting price, which sent me into a rage. When we countered, the guy bailed, and the deal was off the table. Then, I lost my shit for real. As a total rookie at selling a house, I didn't have the wisdom to know that buyers fall through all the time, and when they do, not to fret—the future owner is on the way. At that moment, I just wanted the guy to go to hell. He didn't deserve my house.

The second thing that happened was, I caught wind that the CEO of the toy company was getting ready to cut budgets. As a contractor, I would be the first to go. My income would come to a screeching halt just as we were trying to juggle two houses and slowly chisel away at some of our debt. To my HR friend's credit, she graciously gave me 60 days' notice to get my ducks in a row.

Even though the budget cuts and my departure from the toy company was not a reflection of my performance or contribution, so I was told, my ego took another serious hit. Mentally, I flew back to where I had been months earlier when faced with going back to corporate or taking my business to the next level. The (really heavy) financial burden of the two houses and the plan for Lucas all started to crash down on me. We seemed to be digging ourselves into an even deeper hole.

Anxiety Tipping Point

When Andres and I arrived in San Miguel for our beautiful trip and the gathering of far-flung friends, I was the person that other people didn't want to be around. Unable to put my anxiety aside—even in a magical place with our nearest and dearest—I was consumed with the house situation. Any positive or interesting thoughts or remarks were overshadowed by panic, fear, anger, and worry. If anyone looked at me with the slightest bit of concern in their eyes, I would burst into tears. I could just imagine my friends saying, "God loves that woman but avoid her at all costs or she will corner you and vomit her emotions and stress all over you. Stay away. Save yourself." And though I was aware of my assholishness, I felt powerless to stop it. It was bad.

> ...though I was aware of my assholishness, I felt powerless to stop it.

One afternoon, my friend Alice and I went to get a massage. It was the only time in my life that I cried through half of the rub down. When it was over, we met in our robes in the lounge. I was still crying. Alice reached over to me and said, "This is not our Carrie. This is not you at all. You must call your doctor and get on some meds. You need help. It's okay to need help."

We all need friends who can speak so frankly that it penetrates the brain fog. In that moment, Alice was my angel. She got through. From Mexico, I called my doctor, told her, "No, I'm not suicidal," but I recognized the symptoms from when I had been on anxiety medication twice before in my life, and I needed it again. Wellbutrin would be waiting at CVS pharmacy when I got home.

For the rest of the trip, I tried really hard (without much success) to have fun. I was physically there but I was mentally at home—worried about houses, expenses, and the impending loss of income.

Andres' demeanor was cool like Fonzie, at least on the outside. As the CFO of our household, he had a more robust view of the actual situation combined with his characteristically long-play futuristic view on life. I'm sure he often had his own level of stress in his office late at night but he didn't emotionally express it to the level that I had mastered. But I couldn't ignore the fact that the money coming in was less than money going out. The upcoming black and red reality was sending me to an anxiety tipping point.

When we returned from San Miguel, we switched realtors and our new guy went hard-core. One of the best gifts he gave me was when he told me—not asked, *told* me—that I was not to monitor the showings anymore. I was to stand on the sidelines and wait for any and all updates from him. And I was to ignore the Ring Doorbell. He saw the control freak in me, and he put her in her place, thank the Sweet Lord Baby Jesus.

> **He saw the control freak in me, and he put her in her place.**

Within a week, we had another offer. This time, I just knew it would work out. This was it; the one we'd been waiting for. Even though this offer was less than the first one, the new buyer accepted our counter. I was so ecstatic; I took myself out for a margarita to celebrate and relax. But then, on the very last day of the option period, the buyer pulled out of the contract due to funding, and I went absolutely bonkers.

Up until this point, I'd had one panic attack before in my life and felt another on its way. If you've had one, you know they're not fun. They're awful, as a matter of fact. The first one happened the night before we took Lucas home from the hospital right after he was born. The movie, *A Perfect Storm*, was playing on the TV in my hospital room and took my brain to a dark place. All of the sudden, filled with self-doubt as a new mom, I was frozen with insecurity and terrified that I would accidently hurt my baby or do something stupid. There was likely also a subconscious haze around financially supporting a family of three on my income alone when we were still in debt. Andres was getting angel investment traction for his start-up, but Series A funding was years away.

So, when the second offer on our house fell through, I went straight into all of my barely concealed anxiety, fear and worry—the perfect environment for a super-not-fun panic attack. It came on fast and furious.

Excusing myself early from the office (with my HR friend's blessing) for the day, I walked into our new rental house crying uncontrollably and unable to catch my breath. My chest hurt, I was alone, and all I could think about was that I needed to talk to someone who could calm me the fuck down. I was still trying to get my anxiety under control with the Wellbutrin but clearly it had not kicked in to its full potential. My mind followed the white rabbit down the hole, and in that moment, the white rabbit was shame.

Why did we let ourselves get into such a seemingly endless financial pickle? And how was Andres able to stay so calm while I was a total wreck? I didn't want to burden him with my emotional roller coaster, so I called Ali, my best friend from college. When he heard my faint, breathless voice, he was scared too, and immediately said, "Carrie...breathe. Just breathe, Babe. I'm here...breathe." And so I did. For five minutes, he guided my breathing and calmed me down over the phone. It was a very low point, and I was on the brink of giving up.

> **My mind followed the white rabbit down the hole, and in that moment, the white rabbit was shame.**

Desperately Seeking a Safety Net

As the pressure and stress of our financial situation grew, I had to admit that, ultimately; I was looking for stability in a vast sea of uncertainty. It was clear to me that Andres and I had a stubbornness that was costing us dearly. Neither of us wanted to give up certain aspects of our lifestyle. I struggled to admit that to myself because I wanted to rationalize it, manage the financial pain, and do whatever it took to find any sort of relief. Even if that meant finding stability and security down a path I really didn't want to go down.

My energy level was almost depleted, our house remained unsold, and the reality of our situation was impossible to shove under the rug. After losing the toy company gig and for the second time in a calendar year, I put one foot on the "go back to corporate" track, and the other on the "entrepreneurial build CareerFrame" track, which I was not willing to abandon.

Tapping into my travel network, my resume landed in an interested party's hands along the corporate track. By the end of September, an official corporate job offer was forthcoming. My heart and head were at battle because my heart was screaming "CareerFrame" and my head was screaming "stability," which at the time was only available on the corporate path. My energy to search for another consulting opportunity was practically nonexistent.

> **My heart and head were at battle because my heart was screaming "CareerFrame" and my head was screaming "stability."**

After several months of negotiation—as the bills continued to stack up (and I was not able to contribute)—the travel company and I finally landed on a compensation package that would be "enough." By enough, I mean to say it was not amazing and less than I had made in years but it would suffice. Feeling defeated and badly wanting to stop our financial bleeding, while mentally kicking and screaming from anger and disappointment, I took the offer and agreed to start in December, which was the start date given to me after the back-and-forth negotiations.

Prior to the new corporate job officially starting, we borrowed an embarrassing amount of money from my dad who never once complained, condescended, insulted, or questioned the loan. I assured him that every penny would be paid back in full, and I kept my promise. Though he and my mom divorced when I was just one and my sister Kristen was four-and-a-half, my dad has always had our backs. Whatever we needed, he was there to help. I think he might have literally been a knight in shining armor in a past life because he nails that role in this one. He certainly stepped in to rescue me from the financial stress I was drowning under in this moment.

As I was doing the offer dance with my soon-to-be new employer, our realtor called with some interesting news. The woman who'd made the second offer was back. She was coming into an inheritance but there had been a delay out of her control, hence why she had to back out of the initial offer. Once it came through, she would be golden. We negotiated to give her a lengthy contract to closing period, with the goal to have it wrapped up by the end of the year. This time, I was over it; too tired and worn out from the stress of it all. The sale would either come to fruition or it wouldn't. Either way, I wanted to move on and let the cards fall as they may.

In early December, we moved the rest of our belongings into the rental house. Lucas was settled at his new school, I had the corporate job nailed down, and Christmas was coming. At last, I allowed myself to relax and enjoy the holiday.

On December 28, a large sum of money came into our bank account when our old house officially sold. We got to enjoy it for about five seconds before turning it over to MasterCard. And so began the balancing act between doing what was responsible while still living our lives.

Find Your Juicy Life

Panic is not to be ignored.
Panic is the struggle of the soul when we ignore what it's screaming at us to hear and do. When we are in a state of panic, absolutely nothing useful or productive happens. The desired end will not be reached sooner through panic. In fact, the opposite is true. Be mindful of when panic is ready to attack and build the mental and emotional tools to fight it, head on. As Jen Sincero says, in one of my all-time favorite books, *You Are A Badass*, "Worrying is praying for things you don't want." We attract what we focus on. Tell panic to fuck off. You've got this.

Do not fear the meds.
Thankfully, we are at a time in history where if we need help and it happens to be in a pill, we can get it. I know many moms who refuse to take anxiety or depression medications because of the (limiting) stigma of it. If you are in a state of anxiety and/or depression, please talk to your doctor about your options. There are natural alternatives as well, such as CBD oil and ashwaganda. Don't let shame have a voice when it comes to helping yourself, even if it's through a prescription medication.

Listen to your friends.
The friends who tell you what you *need* to hear, even when you haven't asked, are the keepers: listen to them. Alice's advice was unsolicited, but she saw something I was in no state to see myself. Very gently, she tough loved my ass with some advice that couldn't be ignored. Be mindful of friends and how they read you, showing their true level and depth of friendship, by forcing you to get help when you really need it.

CHAPTER 3

THE BALANCING ACT

"No one can make you feel inferior without your consent."
– Eleanor Roosevelt

The Remark that Lit a Spark

Going back to work full time was not something I was immediately excited about doing but it was the responsible thing to do for my family. Though putting CareerFrame on the back burner was hard (okay fine, it was soul crushing), my dream wasn't dead in the water. I tried to keep my toe in with one-off trainings here and there, but the truth is, I watched it fade into a tiny dot on the horizon, as I reset my sights on doing "the right thing."

Just prior to starting my new corporate position in travel, a well-intentioned, always full of love family member tossed an uninvited observation my way. My mom's younger sister, "AV" as I call her, said, "You know, Carrie, you just aren't where I thought you would be at 43."

Stunned, I attempted to remove the verbal fist from my gut, and snarkily replied, "Where exactly did you think I'd be? Living your life?"

AV is an exceptional woman. Ever elegant, ever classy, impeccable taste, out-of-this-world vocabulary, beautifully decorated homes, generous like no other, and is a fierce mama bear to those she loves, to name only a few characteristics. She cares about me deeply and *only* wants the best for me—I know she does—and at that moment, her comment landed with a shitty delivery.

Emotionally for me, her timing sucked, too. In my strong opinion, she had no understanding of my reality. Although we are very close, have a unique "mother/daughter" bond, and are alike in many ways (and my friends and family love when I impersonate her to perfection), there are quite a few differences between us that led to my reaction in the moment. To name just a few, she wasn't a start-up wife, or had worked a day in corporate with a job that demanded traveling, or supported a family on her single income and just barely, or had a child diagnosed with learning differences and labels, or had the pressures of debt hovering on the daily. To my knowledge, outside of when she and my uncle were newlyweds with no kids and managing low cash flow, fortunately money has almost never been an issue for her in her adult life as my uncle's career took off as a highly successful businessman and CFO.

In addition, once her kids left and she stared into her empty nest, she launched a successful jewelry business and is brilliant with managing her investments. She certainly had her own demands with her previous full-time job as a stay-at-home mom of three kids in the 80s and 90s, juggling the many balls and demands that come along with it while also emotionally supporting a busy, executive husband. And from where I was standing at that moment hearing her choice words, I thought how could she possibly understand why I was where I was?

She responded to my question by saying, "I just expected more for you and from you. I thought you'd own your house and be able to stay home with the kids. I don't like how you're going back to work. You work too hard. You're carrying too much, and it's just not fair. I want you to have a better life."

Although well intentioned and again full of love, care, and concern, to me in that moment, these comments landed very badly. Instead of feeling positive, they came across as a bit insulting (more to my husband than to me with the "stay at home" comment insinuating he wasn't making an income to support that), a bit condescending (with a judgmental tone), somewhat thoughtless (because she couldn't seem to fathom why I might *want* a career), and tone deaf about all I was facing while trying to be responsible for my family.

My internal dialogue launched into overdrive. Silently simmering, I fumed, "Sure, we're renting now but what about the fact that we owned a house for 10 years? Does that not count for anything all of a sudden? And what is wrong with renting a house? And just because we don't have flowers in the yard (like you) because I refuse to put money into plants right now, are we failing at life? And just because *you* wouldn't choose to do what Andres and I have chosen to do, does that make it wrong?"

I went into instant pissed-off defensive mode. Regardless of her "I want the best for you" intentions, the fact, and necessity, that I was working to help make ends meet seemed to almost be completely lost on her through her word choice; at least that's what it felt like.

AV has a fierce love for me and again, we have a uniquely strong bond. She has always mothered me and tells my sister and me often that we are "like her own and her first two babies." She promised my mom before she died that she would take care of Kristen and me, ensure we had enrichments in life, and grow up to be well-mannered, educated, happy, and healthy ladies. She generously over-delivered on this promise and continues to, more so than most relatives ever would. She would have raised us outright if she had been given the chance.

It would be hard to imagine life without AV. As I've grown up, my appreciation for all she has done for me has grown immensely, and it continues to everyday, as life experiences help me to understand the real intentions behind her words and actions. Behind them all is love, there always has been and always will be. Her past traumas and loss fueled her intensity for insisting on my well-being and happiness, and I may not ever be able to truly show her the level of gratitude she deserves. She's one of the boldest women I know, and she will never hold back on telling me what she really thinks. She just may not like when I respond with what **I** really think, especially if our thoughts are not aligned. As we both grow together, we appreciate and respect each other's viewpoints more and more. And, our relationship and love grows stronger overall. Maybe she would feel more comfortable if I lived a life that looked more like hers, which in my eyes is the epitome of freedom. And because I wasn't, I allowed her to make me feel less-than.

Her remarks infuriated me and yet, after sleeping on it, something inside of me woke up—a competitive fire that was all "HELLLL NO!" I didn't need to explain myself to someone who had a very different reality than my own. And at the same time, I did ultimately have to admit I absolutely wanted her lifestyle, and she wasn't wrong with her bold statement about me not being where perhaps I should have been at 43. More accurately, I wanted that financial freedom like she had and to be in control of my own schedule so I could put my kids first, any hour of any day. Her remark lit a spark inside of me that perhaps only she could have ignited. It only magnified my desire for Andres and me to be debt-free and to be able to buy whatever house we wanted; when the time was right, when the kids were out of elementary school, and we no longer needed to live in a specific geographical bubble. I would even want flowers in the front yard.

I loved her *intentions* behind everything she said. I also wanted to smack her when she said them because how dare she (sarcasm) hold up a mirror to show me where I was (or wasn't) in my life. I know why she said what she did. She's always only wanted extraordinary things for me, and quite possibly, it was causing her some sort of pain to watch me "settle" in her eyes. One thing is for sure; she is the definition of unapologetic with her comments and actions.

The truth is, I hadn't put much thought into where I was at 43. I'd been focused on surviving, getting my son where he needed to be, and checking financial boxes. Overall, her comment lit a fire that I didn't realize needed to be lit.

The conversation lit that fire in my belly to be more intentional about what I wanted. It woke me up and it helped to clear a path for me to see where I needed to direct my life. In hindsight, I'm glad she said what she said. Even hurtful comments in the moment can influence a person in the right direction. It fueled my engine to do what was responsible in real time while keeping an eye on where I was determined to end up in the future.

Once I realized the gift she had given me, I could do something about it. But just then, I had a job to do.

Even hurtful comments in the moment can influence a person in the right direction.

Letting Go of "Just So"

At my new corporate gig, I jumped into learning the business and traveling to meet clients and my remote team. The people were truly amazing and welcoming, and never once did I run into someone I didn't genuinely like and/or get along with splendidly. My first business trip was to Miami to meet my boss (who I really liked) in person and dive into an overview of the company, clients, our mission, team expectations, and the like.

After three years, I admit it was a relief to be back in the familiar travel space in a leadership role where I had a sense of professional responsibility and made an impact. Despite an unshakeable feeling of failure around my coaching business and the knowledge that CareerFrame was somewhere "out there" in the distance, it was wonderful to feel important and needed again.

During those few years of staying home, as Chief Household Officer, I was in charge of my babies' routines and grew accustomed to having things be "just so" around the house. Traveling again for work meant being thrust into the reality that other people would be taking care of my kids while I was gone, namely Andres and my mother-in-law, Marta, who came up from Houston to help (my kids lovingly call her Aba, short for Abuela).

When I got home from Miami, some shit got real. I couldn't help myself and—without awareness or understanding—went into being a critic of all that had happened (or didn't happen) while I was gone. Why was I coming home to a messy kitchen? What do you mean the laundry hasn't been done? Did the kids get to bed on time? What were they fed? Why weren't the right snacks sent in their backpacks to school? And on and on.

As the interrogation continued, Andres stopped me and said something that a) I'll never forget, and b) he will never say again, given my reaction. In his defense, he was responding to my accusatory tone and totally overwhelmed by my assault.

With a stern look and voice, he said, "Honey, I did the best I could do. I had to do my day job and YOUR job with the kids while you were gone."

That's when I lost my shit.

"MY JOB? Oh, the kids are MY job? I see. Let me be crystal fucking clear. The day you told me I had to go back to corporate was the day the kids became OUR job! I worked full time all of last year with CareerFrame, and took care of the kids but wasn't traveling. Now I'm working full time and traveling again. You are going to have to step up and take care of the kids with me!"

Now, it's not lost on me that, looking back, Andres never told me to go back to corporate. He told me we needed me to bring in a steady income. I was the one who chose what felt like the safe and secure route. I was the one who simply lacked the energy and confidence to make CareerFrame a legit income-producing business at the time.

That said: this exchange was a pivotal moment in our marriage. My husband realized the weight of the words that had come out of his mouth and accepted that I was right. The kids would need to be OUR job, as long as we were both working full time for companies where we reported up to other leadership, in his case, a Board of Directors.

From that day forward, we were more diligent with our calendars, who was traveling when, and lined up support to help Andres whenever I was away. My husband is beyond capable and, quite frankly, I see him being a dad with our kids more than I see some other dads being. The fact that he is a busy CEO means he needs to have back-up help when I'm gone.

It Takes a Village

Aba has always been happy to come from Houston to help us with Lucas and Lala, as mentioned, but we didn't want to take advantage of her generosity, let alone make her feel like a yo-yo asking her to accommodate my busy travel schedule. When Andres' mother couldn't make it, my cousin Sally came to the rescue. Many times, she enthusiastically and graciously came to stay with our kids and spoiled them rotten. I have no idea how much candy they had when Cousin Sally was in charge, and I don't care. They adored her and had a blast when she was with them. And, they were always happy, with a sugar high, and alive when I returned.

So as not to burn out the good graces of our families, we needed somewhat steady childcare, as a couple coming and going. Thankfully, I have a wife and personally, I think every mom needs one: a person who gets you, predicts your needs, takes the load off your shoulders, is ready to take the kids at any time, doesn't judge you or give unsolicited advice, and helps juggle all the balls you have in the air.

My wife's name is Lynne. I met her in 2013 through Care.com when Lala was 9 months old and I was still working full time at home. She showed up at our house on a freezing cold, icy day in December. The fact that she came for the interview in such conditions was the first hint of her dependability. I hired her immediately.

Lynne was our fifth nanny in three years. The frustrating thing was that only life circumstances kept us from having longer engagements with our previous nannies. One became a teacher, one left to have a baby of her own, one moved out of town, and one was simply unreliable. I often wonder how much easier things would have been if I'd found Lynne first and had one dependable, reliable, and consistent wife in my life. Alas, I found her when I did, and she proved to be all of those things.

When we first met, I was planning to leave Sabre to be a full-time mom, so I was grateful she agreed to a temporary three-month gig. After I stopped working, Lynne stayed on rotation as our trusted, go-to babysitter, and she even boomeranged back a couple of days a week when I needed her the following year. Eventually, she went on to support another family who offered her a steady 60-hour week, but the loyal Ms. Lynne unconditionally loves my babies and has *always* been there for us in a pinch.

As she often reminds me, "to know her is to love her," and she's right! It's beyond comforting to have a trusted person I don't have to explain anything to. She knows the drill with my kids and anticipates all of our needs. Always two steps ahead, she takes care of things before they are articulated, and sometimes even, thought. She is still my go-to babysitter and, because Andres and I are a social couple, she's been there all of these years, caring for the kiddos when our marriage needs one-on-one social time and date nights.

It's beyond comforting to have a trusted person I don't have to explain anything to.

Without Lynne, Sally, Aba, and many other friends and family members around, going back to corporate would have been 10 times more stressful than it was. I never had to worry that things were running smoothly when I was away. I knew my kids were happy and taken care of and that Andres had the space and time to do what he needed to do for his work. Sure, their routine was not the same as the one I had crafted during my time at home, but having my core care team in place was worth its weight in gold.

Long Distance Two Stepping

About four months into my new job, Andres and I took the kids to Cabo San Lucas for spring break. Cabo has a very special place in our hearts. Not only did Andres grow up going there almost annually with his parents; it's where he proposed to me in July of 2006.

Most of the four and a half years that we dated before getting married were long distance. We met two weeks before he left for grad school in Boston through mutual friends, who brought each of us as their wingman to a country and western dance hall in Arlington, Texas, called Cowboys. We all worked for Sabre at the time. Andres was on the corporate side and I was at Travelocity. I remember the moment I saw him, leaning against the bar in tan Wranglers, a heavily starched white shirt, and a big ole cowboy hat, holding a Shiner Bock beer. He had a huge smile beaming through his Van-Dyke goatee. I had just moved back from New York and had been looking for love in all the wrong places. We mingled, danced, and hit it off, so I asked him out to a Lenny Kravitz concert the night before he was leaving for Boston.

The night of the concert, he picked me up at AV's, where I was house sitting upon my recent move back to Dallas. We still laugh about his wardrobe choice that night: a button-up short sleeve shirt tucked into black shorts with a belt, black socks and black shoes. The New Yorker in me eyed him slowly up and down and thought, "Oh no, this outfit! The black socks! This is Lenny—freaking—Kravitz we are seeing. What a NERD!" I managed to move past it and we ended up having a great time.

At the end of the evening, he dropped me off at my aunt's house and kissed me goodnight on my cheek. (Yes, my cheek!) At the time, it was shocking to me how shy and respectful he was. I thought, "Is this what nerds do? They actually respect a woman and go slow? If so, I want one!" We could work on the black socks.

That night, I loaned him my Lenny Kravitz *Greatest Hits* CD and gave him a pencil that I had used to hold my long hair up in a bun. I said, "Good luck at Harvard. Ace all of your tests!" The next morning, Andres drove to Boston listening to my Lenny CD with the pencil sliding back and forth across his dashboard, where it would continue to slide for the next two years.

From day one, Andres was absolutely nothing like anyone I had ever dated. He was tall and skinny (and nerdy, did I already say that?), a Latino from Argentina, wicked smart, and on his way to Harvard Business School—a far cry from the white bread frat guys I dated in college or the fair share of losers in high school. Intrigued as I was, Andres was incredibly introverted and at times for me, painfully quiet. I was sure he would be discouraged by my past or scared by my extroversion.

When he left for Boston, we were realistic about the circumstances but stayed in touch. We spoke occasionally and saw each other with groups of friends whenever he came back to Dallas. We knew we had a connection, but both understood and expected that the other was dating around in our respective cities and that Andres would be having the much-deserved time of his life at grad school.

For two years, our flirtation and relationship continued to grow. I went to Boston to visit, or he came to Dallas. While he got his MBA, I continued to work at Travelocity as the Regional Manager for the Caribbean. (When people saw my title, they had zero empathy for "all of the traveling I had to do.") Through Sabre flight benefits with American Airlines, we would meet up in Vegas, Aruba, the Bahamas, Costa Rica and other destinations.

As romantic and dreamy as all of this may sound, it was a weird time of uncertainty. Due to our schedules and Andres' focus on school, we weren't able to talk on the phone that often and I wasn't at all sure where things were heading.

On a spring day during his last semester, Andres called. I was on my way to an Aruba Tourism party on the beach. He wanted me to be the first to know he had accepted a post-grad-school position with Sabre, and this time, at Travelocity. I was over the moon happy. Right up until he said it was in the West Palm Beach, Florida office.

At that moment, I had immense conflict: happiness for him and utter disappointment for myself. Two years filled with questions about how he really felt about me was turning into another long-distance marathon for Lord only knew how long but we decided to officially commit to each other and continue the routine.

For the next two years, our relationship escalated. The ultimate test was when we went on our first serious trip together to Singapore, Sri Lanka and Thailand. It was a three-week experience like none I've ever had (to this day) and it pretty much sealed the deal. We were beyond compatible traveling together, and for two people in the travel industry, that was huge.

While we were away, a recruiter from Google reached out to me about a senior position in the Dallas office. After six months of interviews, I was offered the job, accepted, and put my foot down with Andres. One of us was going to have to move, and it was not going to be me.

In fairness, I had contemplated uprooting to South Florida to make the relationship work in person. However, it was the last place I wanted to live. In hindsight, if I had moved there, we probably wouldn't have survived. The pressure and my potential neediness—in a place where I knew no one and didn't want to be—would have put too much strain on the situation. And, one of the many things Andres loves about me is my independence and confidence.

> **One of us was going to have to move, and it was not going to be me.**

He heard me loud and clear and made some internal calls at Travelocity. As fate would have it, the perfect position for him became available in Dallas. On April 1 of 2006, Andres' car was delivered to the driveway of my duplex, and I picked him up at the airport that evening. Thankfully, for my heart, it was not an April Fool's joke.

Three months later, he took me to Cabo San Lucas and told me we would be staying at his parent's timeshare. A uniformed gentleman in a Mercedes greeted us at the airport. I looked at Andres and said, "Some timeshare you have!" Thirty minutes later, we arrived at Las Ventanas, one of the most exquisite resorts in all of Mexico. My immediate thought was "Oh. My. God. If he doesn't propose to me here, in this magical place, I will lose my shit."

To my hope and (yet still) surprise, two nights later—completely calm, cool, collected, confident, handsome as ever, and with no black socks in sight—he got on bended knee on the beach, pulled a bottle out of the sand that was buried next to a fire pit, slid a letter out of the bottle, and read it to me. The last sentence was: will you marry me? As a bonus, he presented me with a diamond to die for, and of course, I said yes.

We were married 10 months later on February 24, 2007. Over 200 friends and family from many parts of the world came for the most incredible party that lasted until 8 a.m. the following day. At our rehearsal dinner, he confessed to everyone that he knew he would marry me the night we met at Cowboys all those years earlier. I lovingly yelled at him, "Hey!! A heads-up on that about three years ago would have been SUPER helpful, ya bastard!" I should have known when he chose to spend his last night with me before he left for Boston; he saw something bigger for us. Years later, when we found out we were having a son, we decided to name him Lucas as a shout out to where our family began with that proposal.

Whereas my husband is still introverted and set in his nerdy ways, I find it all endearing now. He came into his own style, often times more presentable than me, dressed sharply with every head and beard hair in place. He's my "beefy" husband who gets better with age. He has come out of his shell more and more over the past almost 20 years since I've influenced and beat him down, I mean, known him. Let's face it, being married to a raging extrovert has taught him to appreciate our opposites, or just simply shake his head, give up, and love my crazy. Even when we have our introvert vs. extrovert fights, we always learn from them and come out stronger.

I often tell him that there are not enough amazing adjectives in the dictionary to describe him—full of integrity, honesty, thoughtful of others, a true gentlemen, incredible dad, and outstanding husband. Through all of my insecure, psycho, overly emotional, and complaining moments, he has stood steadfast like a rock, never fleeing, always positive, and loving me like I've never been loved.

I'm often asked how we made four-plus years of long-distance dating work. The simple, anticlimactic answer is: we were meant to be. Long distance was hard, really hard some days, but the universe had plans for us the night we met, and we are still two-stepping our way through a wonderful marriage and partnership. Andres is quite simply an amazing human being and my teacher on this crazy, juicy thing called life. I'm honored he asked me along for the ride.

Globe Trotting Groove Train

The Cabo trip with the kids was an opportunity to exhale, though I still juggled work responsibilities while away. I was grateful to have a boss who told me to run, not walk, to spring break with the family despite only being in the job for four months, and I wanted to show her I was committed and focused. She and the other people in the organization truly understood that living life was more important than being at work, as long as the work still got done.

Months flew by in the new job as I plane hopped and traveled to meet clients and team members. I was able to settle into a routine, my family was in a groove, and I told myself that things were going well. After 15-plus years on the consumer side of travel, I grew more and more acquainted with the corporate side of the business, which was arguably not nearly as "sexy." But the stability and certainty of it was appreciated and necessary.

Our household debt was still much too high to admit or tackle and yet, travel opportunities started to pop up like mad. But we were not going to sit and dwell in our situation. We were going to work through it while living life. Using points and miles wherever we could, Andres and I took advantage of as many of the trips that popped up as we could. We needed personal, couple's time away for us to connect after the turmoil of the year before. Plus, I'm at home when I'm traveling, especially with Andres. It's a peaceful zone for me full of fun, different cuisines, and time together, whenever I can disconnect from my anxiety. I missed my babies but with our core care team in place, in addition to my amazing sister saving our asses on multiple occasions as well, I knew they were in good hands, and my daily phone calls held them over until we returned.

Our travels took us to Puerto Rico on a friend's yacht, two different friends' weddings in Cartagena, Colombia, Sonoma (nothing calms the soul like winery hopping), and a surprise trip for the kids to Disneyland. We wanted to take them the year before but didn't because, believe it or not, there was some sane financial responsibility along the way. Now, the corporate job made it possible.

Taking all of those ancillary trips back-to-back was not remotely financially responsible with the mountain of debt we faced. I know this. But frankly, sometimes, I didn't care. We wanted and needed to get away. Knowing a secure paycheck was in flow, I could breathe, relax and enjoy. Or so, I told myself.

Find Your Juicy Life

Get a wife.
It doesn't matter if you are married, have a partner, or are single: if you have kids, you need a wife. Finding a partner that you trust who is not related to you (but who feels like family without the strings attached) is the biggest gift you can give yourself and your kids. A mom wife will keep you sane, and save you when you need saving but are afraid to ask.

Live your life.
My revised version of Jack's famous saying is, "All work and no play makes Jane a dull, anxiety-riddled, short-fused, unfulfilled mom!" Take care of what's necessary and recognize that sometimes, you need to have fun for the hell of it. I will never encourage someone to go into debt or add to an existing debt because being in debt sucks. But I will encourage moms to pay attention to what really matters, and find whatever wiggle room they can to do what juices them up.

CHAPTER 4

GRIEF WILL ROCK YOU

"My soul is painted like the wings of butterflies. Fairy tales of yesterday grow but never die. I can fly, my friends."
– Freddie Mercury

The Day the Music Died

Bohemian Rhapsody, the definitive and Academy Award winning film about Freddie Mercury and Queen, came out in October of 2018. A friend in Washington D.C. invited me to a studio sneak preview when I was in the city on business. I've always been fascinated by Freddie Mercury, and was eager and ready to see the film. However, I was not ready for what it triggered.

After the movie, we went back to my friend's house for a glass of wine. Standing in her kitchen, I said, "Well, that was amazing. And here, I'm gonna go."

"What do you mean?" she asked. "Where are you gonna go?"

"I know me. I'm going down a total immersion, Freddie Mercury/Queen rabbit hole. Now, I have to learn everything about him, and I know I'm going to get all weird and OCD about it, just like I did when Michael Jackson died."

She laughed, not comprehending the depths to which I'd go.

I'll never forget when I got the news about Michael Jackson's death in 2009. I was sitting outside at a quaint wine bar in Brooklyn with my friend, Karina. My other bestie, Gina, who knows how hard I take celebrity deaths (which I totally do) and didn't want to be the one to tell me about MJ, bravely called to break the news anyway.

My immediate response was, "Holy shit! Well… If you were calling to tell me Tom Hanks had died, forget it. That would send me over the edge. But MJ, don't worry; I'm not going to get upset. I'm shocked but I'm fine. Sad though, he was a musical genius!"

Sidebar: whenever someone says something is *fine*, it's not even remotely fine. Why I thought hearing about his death would be "*fine*" is beyond me, especially because of what Michael Jackson signified in my early childhood.

Over the next couple of days, Michael's music poured out of every open window, bar, and shop in New York City. I may or may not have busted out my best Billie Jean leg kick and fedora-hat head-cock a few times, in tribute to the King of Pop.

When I got back to Dallas, the news of his death began to sink in, and I started digesting every news report on his death, his estate, his funeral plans, everything—on a daily basis. I bought every magazine with him on the cover and listened exclusively to MJ songs, including the Jackson 5, on incessant repeat. When his funeral was broadcast live from the Staples Center in Los Angeles, I stayed glued to the TV as his gold casket was rolled into the arena and John Mayer played "Human Nature" (my favorite Michael Jackson song) on guitar. For two hours, legends like Stevie Wonder, Mariah Carey, Smokey Robinson and Lionel Ritchie paid tribute to his life.

The next day, I fell into a depression. Watching the funeral and consuming myself with Michael Jackson's death was oddly like reliving the loss of my mom. She got sick when I was 5, and she died three weeks after my 9th birthday. The light in my eyes, the excitement in my heart, the skip in my step, and all of my creativity died, too.

> **...consuming myself with Michael Jackson's death was oddly like reliving the loss of my mom.**

I spoke to an Intuitive one time who told me I was living life from a 5-year-old's operating system. Her observation made a lot of sense. I've always been a fast talker, fast mover, non-stop, constantly on-the-go person. The Intuitive was not surprised to hear this. She suggested the 5-year-old girl inside of me was still "running" from her pain so it wouldn't catch up to her. I imagine I buried all the fear, sadness, worry, stress, anger, uncertainty, and every other emotion from that time as deep down into my subconscious as I could dig, never to be found again. And because I never addressed this—or even realized it—a wounded little girl had been steering the ship of my entire life.

My mother, Nancy Jane Michaelis Davis Bourn, was an amazing woman. I was glued to her, in awe of her, totally in love with her. She was a private investigator (Nancy Bourn, P.I.). I'd say, "Mommy, you're just like Magnum," referencing Tom Selleck's iconic 80s TV show.

My memories of her are sadly few and far between but the ones I cherish involve Motown music, Michael Jackson, Elton John, Hall & Oats, margaritas, cigarettes, puzzles, Vitabaths, dancing in the living room to Macho Duck and Duran Duran, trips to the doll store, a flower corsage delivered to me at school on my birthday, and a lot of concerts.

My mom took my sister Kristen and me to every concert that came to Austin, Texas, where we lived. My first concert with her was the Bee Gees at age 6. To this day, I cannot hear "Stayin' Alive" without thinking of her. One time, when she was too sick to take us, my mom dispatched my stepdad, Joe, to take us to the Men at Work concert, and rock out to vegemite sandwiches in the land down under. A man who preferred classical music, Joe was such a trooper, and sat through the entire show, eating a tub of popcorn, in pop concert hell, while Kristen and I sang and danced our hearts out.

> ... a wounded little girl had been steering the ship of my entire life.

But, of all of those memories and for all her musical influences, Michael Jackson is the most synonymous with memories of my mother. My whole life, I've never been able to hear any Michael Jackson song without her immediately coming into my thoughts, no matter where I am or what I'm doing. She was obsessed with his music. I remember watching him on TV do the moonwalk during the Motown 25 special in 1983 from her bed in my parent's room. My mom was freaking out, yelling, "Oh my god! What is he doing? Look at him! Whooo hooo, go Michael!" Nine months later, she would be gone.

When MJ died, all of the memories—of us dancing to his music, listening to his songs in the car and singing them out loud, watching him do the moonwalk, bringing home *The Thriller* album—came flooding back, and with them came a deep, painful, longing ache for her.

My grief was not even remotely expected or anticipated and yet, here it was, bringing me to my emotional knees. And then, even more unexpected than the sadness, came an overpowering and massive anger at my mom for "leaving me." The little girl in me came out, and she was totally pissed!

For almost eight weeks, I cried, kicked and screamed. I yelled at the air, hoping my mom would hear how mad I was at her for dying. I had to grow up without her! She wasn't at any of the major milestones in my life! She hadn't met my husband, or Lucas, or Lala! Hell, I was even pissed that she wasn't there to pin my Tri Delta pin on me at my sorority initiation, following in her sorority footsteps as a double legacy. Instead, my fellow Tri Delta grandmother had to step in, and I couldn't even exude appreciation to her because she simply wasn't Mom.

Those weeks following MJ's death were filled with short-fused flare-ups directed at anyone who crossed my path. Andres was at a loss. He hugged me, asked if there was anything he could do, and to his credit, he backed off. He let me go through whatever the hell it was I needed to go through. Eventually, the tidal wave subsided into calmer seas. The little girl had finally grieved for what she had been through.

> The little girl in me came out, and she was totally pissed!

The Show Must Go On

After *Bohemian Rhapsody*, my immersive state with Freddie lasted for *eight months*, which made the two-month MJ trance look like a blip. On full-scale overdrive, I read and watched and listened to everything I could get my hands on. I listened to Queen non-fucking-stop. I watched every YouTube video, every interview, literally e-v-e-r-y thing I could find on Freddie. I memorized Queen's Live Aid performance and all the moves Freddie made during each song.

Sidebar: Personally, I think it's awesome that my kids know all the words to "Killer Queen" and "Radio GaGa." I'm pretty sure that for the rest of their lives, much like I think of my mom when I hear Michael, they will think of me when they hear Queen.

Sometime early into the Freddie immersion, the crying started. Day after day, the tears came in waves. And out of the blue, for no apparent reason, they kept coming. The days grew into weeks and weeks into months.

Andres quietly observed my behavior with a raised eyebrow of inquiry. Attempting reassurance, I said, "Hey, I'm okay. I think I know what this is about. Just hug me and love me. Don't try to solve anything. Whatever is happening, I have to go through it. But I think this is about my mom. Again."

I had no association between my mother and Freddie Mercury, or answers as to why exactly a movie about his life was affecting me so violently. Why was I 10 times sadder, more depressed, and grief stricken than I'd been nine years earlier when Michael died?

And then it hit me. Something about Freddie, the fight for his life and his drive to sing, to show up, and to protect his loved ones until the day he died triggered an odd comparison to my mom in my heart. With Michael Jackson, I grieved for the little girl who lost her mother. I was a young, married woman without children of my own yet, so it was all about me. With Freddie Mercury, I grieved *for my mother*: the amazing, beautiful, dynamic, courageous, young woman with two little girls, who faced her own death at just 38 years old.

The only place I was able to grieve from (this time) was as a mom, and for her: the person she was. This grief was overwhelming, devastating, debilitating. I took long Vitabaths to remember how she smelled. I talked to her while I soaked in the tub, submerged in her clean scent. "I cannot even imagine what you were thinking and feeling. You had two young daughters. You didn't like your ex-husband's wife. For all you knew, she would be the one to see your daughters' milestones, plan the weddings, nurture the grandchildren. You were so young. You probably felt the most incomprehensible anger, sorrow, sadness, confusion, pain and fear."

The more I thought about *her* loss, the harder I cried. I have never wanted to go back in time so badly to tell someone something. I wanted to tell her, "Mom, I'm so sorry this is happening to you. I want you to know that Kristen and I are going to be more than okay. Dad is going to step up like you cannot imagine. His wife will eventually move on from his life, so she won't be there for any of *your* moments. Dad is going to be Mr. Mom and take care of us. AV will always be hovering and ensuring we grow up to be young ladies, with great educations and experiences. We are both going to see the world and marry great guys and have the most amazing children who will know all about you. We will miss you, and we will be okay. Release your worry, and go in peace!"

Because I'm not a time traveler, I told the air, I told her gravesite, I told her in prayer, and meditation, and continued grieving for her for several more months. As the cycle neared the end, I started to feel physically lighter. Decades of suppressed grief that the little 5-year-old had been clinging to left my body. I was able to reach a place where I no longer missed my mother from a place of trauma, but from a place of love and honor for who she was in life on this planet.

Interestingly enough, just as I found my smile again and didn't feel the need to listen to Freddie belting that magical voice as much anymore, the date arrived for a concert Andres and I bought tickets to six months earlier:

Queen with Adam Lambert. At the show, I sang my heart out, cheered, danced and didn't shed one tear. I celebrated with my mom instead.

It took two deceased rock/pop legends to release my soul from decades of anguish. Being the music fanatic she was, my mother would have had it no other way. I often imagine my mom found Michael and Freddie in whatever great beyond they are all in, hugged them both, and said, "Thank you for helping my daughter let go of this grief. Now, when I whisper in her ear, she will hear me. Now, when she plays your music, she'll feel that I'm dancing right beside her. When she feels a light breeze touch her face, she'll know it's me and smile."

Intuition Strikes

In the midst of the depths of sadness, and after almost a year of working as a director in corporate travel, I made the decision to attend an exclusive, 12-person "Women in Travel" event in Park City, Utah. My attendance was not associated with my day job, but rather to connect, learn and grow for CareerFrame, my back-burnered baby, my dream off in the distant horizon.

As the event kicked off, we got the chance to mingle and chat with the event speakers, one of whom really caught my attention. Her name was Molly. I spotted her as we went into the restaurant for dinner and hurried over to ask if we could sit together. She willingly agreed.

As we started talking, I found myself sharing some unspoken (and unrealized) feelings with her. In a flash, I realized I had been robotically showing up for work, smiling through the day, leading a team, and doing what I needed to do, but I was completely unfulfilled. I'd been feeling that way all year but hadn't allowed myself to admit or embody it, pushing my instincts down into the shadows, staying focused on what I *had* to do for my family. In this beautiful setting with Molly, the truth bubbled to the top.

"Honestly, I had to take this corporate job to stop the financial bleeding and do the right thing," I confided to her. She immediately put on her coaching hat and said, "Change your words. You didn't HAVE to, you CHOSE to. Be glad that job came along for you; don't resent it."

I had been robotically showing up for work, smiling through the day, leading a team, and doing what I needed to do, but I was completely unfulfilled.

Right then and there, she shifted me. She was right. My internal word choice fueled my discontent. There was no power in them. And so, the next thing that came out of my mouth was a complete surprise. "Can we set up some time to talk? I'm curious about your coaching program."

A week later, I was working remotely from a gorgeous room at the Aria Hotel in Las Vegas, where I'd flown to meet Andres who was attending the Expedia conference. While he was out at meetings, Molly and I hopped on our first, exploratory call. She wanted to get a better understanding of where I was mentally and emotionally and to uncover my "why" for talking with her further. Once she had a sense of where I was coming from, she laid out her "Cracking Open" coaching program, which included three one-on-one sessions a month, two group coaching video calls, and a workbook to record goals and accomplishments. It was offered in three, six, or 12-month commitment blocks. Everything she presented sounded perfect for me until she told me the cost. It was higher than anticipated.

Price tag aside, my heart screamed, "Hell yes! I need this; let's do it!" My lizard brain, entrenched in its scarcity/lack money mindset, piped in to remind me about our debt, and I froze. Lizard brain said, "What the hell are you thinking?! You can't afford this. What a stupid decision. Walk away."

My internal wavering and reluctance to commit came through on the phone with Molly. "Well, it all sounds good. Let me think about it, discuss it with Andres, and I'll be in touch." She understood, and then she gently advised me that investing in myself would always have the highest return on investment. Investing in myself, especially like this, was something I had never done before, nor even contemplated up until this point.

Then, something remarkable happened; something that, to be honest, I don't recall ever happened before. My heart spoke up. It damn near yelled. "EXCUSE. ME! I'm in charge here. Lizard brain, I'd like to lovingly tell you to shut the hell up! I need this. I feel it, and I am listening. I will find a way." My entire body got chills.

Guided by my heart, the next words out of my mouth were, "Actually, I'm not going to think about this. I'm going to act. I want 12 months. I'm all in. Let's do it."

The fact is, shit needed to change. I wanted to get back to my coaching business, and something was telling me to give myself an avenue to get there. I didn't ask Andres' permission and I don't recall asking him to review the agreement Molly sent a few days later, either. This was something I needed for myself. Much like that week alone in London, it was a non-negotiable necessity. It was my turn to focus on me, and this time, it needed to be more intensive than a week in London. I was ready to make a personal investment that would offer a real and meaningful, juicy soul return.

Find Your Juicy Life

Cry until you are done crying.
Don't hold back the crying, or shut it off, or be hard on yourself for crying at all. Seek out someone to talk to about the grief and keep going. In her book, *Sober Curious*, Ruby Warrington uses the analogy of carrying two very full, heavy buckets of water. When you pour some water out, they get lighter. Cry until you feel lighter and cry until the well runs dry. Now, when I cry, I know to look for the meaning behind the tears. Is it anger? Sadness? Frustration? Joy? When you know what you are really crying about, you can address it.

Go all in on yourself.
As Molly reminded me, "Investing in yourself will always give you the highest ROI." We can only grow when we choose to lean in and learn. Often, pain is behind that growth and if we show up for the lesson, pain can be an incredible teacher. If we aren't growing, we're dying. You simply must invest in yourself and nurture your mind and heart with the good juicy stuff that helps you become a livelier version of yourself. Find books that move you, inspire you, teach you, and encourage you to take action to better your life. When you invest in yourself to become who you are meant to be, that's when you can show up for everyone else, especially your little humans who are watching every move you make. Always invest in *you* first.

Find a way with intention.
When life presents you with meaningful challenges, lean into them. Reframe your thinking and consider what that moment has presented to teach you. Instead of "can't-ing" your way through something due to limiting beliefs and fear of the unknown, talk things through and see if you are able to accept the challenge because it's meaningful. When we act because something matters versus act (or not act) out of fear, the domino effect that follows can be downright awe-inspiring. When something matters, tap into courage and find a way.

Lessons Learned through Frustration

When I took that rejuvenating solo trip to London in 2016, I learned one primary, overarching lesson: it is completely okay to put myself first. The experience was the beginning of a massive turning point. Whereas I took heavy burdens with me in regards to the plan for Lucas, how we would make it work, and the fact that I had to step up my income-making potential, I gave myself the space to sort it out on my own with intention. I was unapologetically happy to have alone time for an entire week, and I'm grateful to have a husband who did not stand in my way. When we give ourselves space, we make room for greatness to come in.

As moms, disconnecting from our kids from time to time is a good thing. Hell, it's downright healthy and necessary. We don't love them any less. We don't think about them any less. We simply make and take the opportunity to put ourselves first for five seconds, or five days, or whatever we can manage. Critically, don't feel bad about it. Guilt has no place in putting yourself first because then you are half-assing your self-care.

Back home, however, Andres and I faced some hard financial decisions, the byproducts of which fueled my anxiety. When I look back at the amount of emotional stress I allowed myself to endure, and on many days, flat-out create, I hurt for my younger self. I learned then that life truly is not linear; it's a big squiggly line that goes in every direction, up and down, like the butterfly flies, and then you land where you are meant to. The big goal was to get Lucas into a new school with a special program, and we made it happen.

Everything ends up exactly how it is supposed to, and we miss out on the journey when we try to control every moving part. After *Bohemian Rhapsody*, my grief for my mother brought me to my knees. It looked similar to when Michael Jackson died and the grief for the little girl in me was triggered. And yet, it was fundamentally different. It was profound and deeply cathartic, despite the outward behavior exhibited during those dark months. The unhealed grief in my soul was ready to be unloaded, and when the time came, I had to sit with it.

Telling myself everything was "fine" was not going to help me grow and heal from grief surrounding the loss of my mother or from feeling unfulfilled in my career. Life throws circumstances at you to help you get dark, mucky, black blocks of negative energy out of your body. Pay attention to them, look at who or what is showing up in your life, and respect the emotional process.

Meeting Molly in Park City provided an opportunity to listen to my heart, which was screaming so adamantly, I had to listen, no matter what my head said. When you are preparing for a climb, you start by getting your heart rate up, then you pull back to rest because the big climb is still ahead. For that, you have to be ready, and by the time I met Molly, I was. After two years of feeling like there was so much more to life than what I was living, it was time to go all in.

PART 2
F.E.A.R.

Find. Everything. And. Rise.

CHAPTER 5

CRACKING OPEN

"The most important investment you can make is in yourself."
–*Warren Buffett*

The Island, The Boat & The Rudder

On January 8 of 2019, Molly and I kicked off our coaching journey. Even though I still had no idea how I would afford this commitment, I was ready to dive in and explore who I was, where I had been, and more importantly, where I was heading.

Important to note, a coach is different than a therapist. Whereas both a therapist and a coach allow you time to vent and get things off your chest, a coach kicks your ass into taking action to affect change.

The beauty of Molly was that she was a therapist for decades and transitioned into being an intuition coach, which is someone who specializes in helping people get in touch with the deepest parts of themselves by listening to, and following, their intuition. Working with her meant access to the best of both worlds. Plus, she tells it like it is.

> ... a coach kicks your ass into taking action to affect change.

In my experience, both as a coach and as someone who has been coached, knowing exactly where to start is hard to pinpoint. It's amazing we find the strength and desire to hire a coach to begin with, and when it's time to get to work, we feel like a doe in the headlights, which is totally how I felt.

The first session with Molly did not disappoint. She started by asking questions to set a foundation for where we were headed. I recall sharing that my purpose for hiring her was to get help and support to get back to CareerFrame. We revisited our initial dinner conversation in Park City, and she didn't need to remind me of my comment about "having" to go back to corporate. She immediately understood that I was unhappy and unfulfilled with where I was. My goal was to get to a place of career fulfillment, which for me meant making my own coaching and training business a meaningful and financial success.

I was ready to go, ready to learn, ready to jump into all of the steps I would need to take to get back to business! I pummeled her with questions: What type of infrastructure do I need to set up for the business? Which books did she recommend reading? Was she willing to talk through my strategic plans?

As I laid out all of my ideas and expectations for our coaching engagement, Molly kindly, lovingly and gently laughed. She said, "Carrie, I love your drive. Oh my god, you are such a go-getter, and it's fantastic. However, you do realize that we are likely going to need to start with YOUR infrastructure, right? We need to start with YOU to see what needs to be cracked open personally so you can get out of your own way professionally."

Well... dammit.

The fast-paced activator in me wanted to dive immediately into the desired *outcome*: get the hell out of corporate and back to a consulting career that filled me up. As a coach myself now, I can see that Molly was 1000 percent spot on with where we had to start. I could only get where I wanted to be after I spent some time looking in the mirror and going into the shadows of my subconscious to dig some shit out.

When Molly and I started working together, I was only two months into the eight-month grieving journey for my mother. Even so, somehow I thought we would be focusing on Career Woman Carrie, not Grieving Carrie who had serious personal work to do. I had another thing coming.

Over the next few weeks, we went everywhere with my psyche and heart, diving right into the depths of my limiting belief system, current frustrations, and biggest desires. We paid close attention to my gut reactions to everything I had done in life, and how I handled situations, especially in the two years that led up to our engagement. On occasion, she would guide me through meditations and often gave me homework that consisted of journaling or taking some sort of action.

Molly was responsive to a metaphor I used to describe my situation. Currently, I was in the "corporate boat," sailing my way to CareerFrame Island off in the distance. The corporate gig was my lifeboat of financial stability to get me where I really wanted to be. At that point, I couldn't see the island, but I knew it was there, so I tried to sail my boat in its general direction.

Interestingly, at that same time, a new shiny object grabbed my attention. A travel start-up reached out to gauge my interest in a role. My ego kicked in, and out of the blue, I focused on this gig simply as a means to get a pay raise. Still disgruntled about the "just enough" offer I'd accepted from the corporate job, I felt defeated at "having" to take what amounted to the lowest salary in my leadership career. Molly and I had already discussed my money panic and lack mindset, the debt my husband and I carried, and the fact that our lifestyle did not match our income. After only a year in the corporate gig, my answer was to pursue the start-up job that paid more as a way to chip away at our debt faster.

When I spoke to Molly about it, she asked me what I wanted to make, and I gave her the figure. My homework was to meditate, visualize working at the start-up, stop going out to eat, make chicken soup for dinner, and cancel the cable to kick start other ways of saving while plotting my move to make more income.

That week, I had a weird dream. I was wearing a casual outfit, sitting outside on a swing set under a huge, beautiful tree when I received an email from the founder of the start-up. Super casual and conversational, he wrote to say he'd been given a hot tub and was curious if I was interested in having it. As I was reading the email, he drove up in a black sports car pulling the hot tub on a trailer behind him. Of course, I wanted it but where would I put it? I visualized Andres and myself relaxing in the hot tub and I wondered how much he wanted for it. He never stated the price but we started chatting easily about life and kids. I told myself this was a positive sign about a job offer coming my way: the new boss was stopping by to chat socially and offered something that would make me warm and relaxed. Then I woke up.

The job offer didn't materialize, which like most things, was a blessing in disguise. Maybe the hot tub was my intuition saying I'd be in "hot water" if I took a job primarily for more money. If anything, the experience helped me get over myself and appreciate what I had with the corporate gig. Also, the salary carrot stirred up something deep inside of me around earning potential, and it got me thinking: when is enough really enough?

Molly pointed out that I often got in my own way by "putting the rudder down" in my little boat sailing towards CareerFrame Island. Unsure what she meant by that she clarified, "You need to let gooooo! Let the boat take you where you are meant to go. Stop trying to control everything. Focus on what you want, put your energy towards it, and then simply let go, trust, wait, and watch what happens."

> **...the salary carrot stirred up something deep inside of me around earning potential, and it got me thinking: when is enough really enough?**

I wanted freedom: financial, spiritual, physical, mental, and emotional. I wanted peace and yet, to Molly's point, I kept putting the rudder down. My need for control was getting in my way, big time. As she said, I simply needed to aim the boat and trust that the wind would get me there.

The more I let my life flow, the more energy would flow, and the more I would attract abundance in every aspect (or so I hoped). Then, one day, while sitting in my little metaphorical boat, a nice big gust of wind came to give me a push forward, and Molly was the one who sent it.

Wave After Wave

Two months into working together, Molly gave me the gift of a lead. A client of hers from Seattle was looking for the type of support that someone like me could offer, so Molly put us in touch. We talked, I sent a proposal, and the proposal was accepted. Just like that! I had set a goal to land five CareerFrame gigs in 2019, and here was the first one in the bag. My plan was to use my paid time off to deliver for CareerFrame clients and hang on to the corporate job.

The universe is funny. It tested me, and when I responded the way it wanted me to, it rewarded me. I played back how this reward came to be in my mind. When Molly told me her price for coaching during our initial phone call, my brain said, "freeze," and my heart said, "go for it." My brain was telling me that I had no idea how I was going to pay her rate for this journey, so walk away. My heart wanted me to grow and knew I'd find a way to pay for it. The lead that Molly sent me, which turned into a new client, agreed to pay me the exact same dollar amount that I had agreed to pay Molly for the entire year of coaching. I passed the universal test because the heart wins every time!

The heart wins every time!

Over the next several sessions, Molly and I talked about my job, my family, my past, and how I naturally went into "trauma response" because of my childhood. She was constantly telling me to pace myself because I was always emotionally running, as if I was on speed, so the pain wouldn't catch up to me. Her observation was totally in line with what the Intuitive said about a 5-year-old being in control of my psyche. Molly had an acronym to use in situations where I noticed myself running like a lunatic. She said to H.A.L.T.—if you're Hungry, Angry, Lonely or Tired—do nothing. Slow down, pace yourself, and focus before proceeding.

Molly also encouraged me to give more than to receive. She said that givers are more successful, and if I gave more, I would be able to manifest the life I dreamed of. Manifesting became a big focus for many of our sessions. Even though there were so many things I loved about my current life, she heard me subconsciously crying for something different. I was still unfulfilled career-wise and was still working through wave after wave of unhealed trauma.

Regardless of being a direct and blunt person, there were times when I struggled to say something to a friend, co-worker, or family member. Molly cheered me on to own my shit and my feelings, be transparent, and speak my truth. Every time I did, whatever conversation I'd been dreading or turned into some huge emotional mountain to climb, was always a non-issue and quickly resolved itself.

As an intuition coach, Molly told me to listen to my intuition, which again jibed with an observation the Intuitive had made, when she said, "You are profoundly gifted at manifesting and following your intuition, just as soon as you stop pissing and moaning about everything!" Well, there's that.

With each month that went by, the roller coaster of emotions continued. Molly quickly homed in on helping me identify my primary fear, which is almost always a layer deeper than we think. I had many fears but they all stemmed from one deep, dark, rooted fear.

She pushed me and asked, "What are you afraid of?"

"Failure," I responded.

She said, "No, I don't think that's it. Go deeper."

"Rejection."

"No," she said. "I don't think that's it either. I think you are afraid of loss."

When she said those words, I instantly choked up and almost couldn't talk.

She said, "Sweetie, I think you have been so codependent on suffering from loss that it's keeping you from joy. Loss of your mom, loss of your childhood, loss with other loved ones, loss with money. You are frozen with fear around loss. You are scared that you are going to lose everything, so you hold on tightly with a scarcity mindset when we need to get you to an abundant mindset. You deserve joy and freedom, you are worthy of both, and only an abundant mindset will allow you to have those gifts."

...you have been so codependent on suffering from loss that it's keeping you from joy.

She was raw and she was right. Molly told me what I needed to hear. And now that we had identified my primary fear and pain point, I had to do something about it.

Find Your Juicy Life

Name your island "out there."
Do you have a big dream that's been deferred or back burnered? What are you aiming toward? Having goals, or at least one BHAG (big hairy audacious goal) can be the north star for your future. If you don't know what your North Star is, or should be, don't worry. Keep going, thinking, feeling, asking, and exploring what lights you up and what joy truly means to you. Then aim and go get it. It's out there waiting for you.

Recognize temptations of the ego.
The grass is not always greener. It's greener where you water it. Life throws many shiny objects at us, like the distraction of a potential new job opportunity only one year into my corporate job. Make sure you really think before you jump from the frying pan into the fire. The ego shows up ONLY when we have insecurities about something. Be mindful of when the ego is trying to take you down a rabbit hole.

Identify your root fear.
If you're not aware of what's holding you back, you won't be able to conquer the "real" fear. Real fear is something that will result in something detrimental; it's not real if it's something untrue that your brain is simply making up in order to keep you stuck. Our real fear is almost always layers deeper than the fear we can quickly identify, unless we have already done the work to identify it. The real fear often fuels other fears but until you get to THE fear, your healing will be postponed. Have a trusted friend, therapist or coach prompt you with questions to help you dig deeper, and then ask them to tell you what they hear you saying, as Molly told me. Sometimes we have to have someone else tell us what fear they see and hear is paralyzing us before we can see or hear it ourselves.

CHAPTER 6

THE UNEXPECTED GURU

"Where focus goes, energy flows."
-Tony Robbins

Divine Timing

Six months into my Cracking Open journey with Molly, we had unearthed a healthy pile of pain and trauma, fears and doubts that—up until choosing this path—I'd never really admitted out loud. Great progress was made with several steps forward and few steps back, but regardless I worked to shift some deep-rooted beliefs.

I needed something to happen that would propel me closer to CareerFrame Island, and once again, divine timing was on my side. Andres and I were in the kitchen one night when he casually said, "Hey, I should connect you with my friend George. He's from our Burning Man camp, and he just started working for Tony Robbins. He's into the same coaching stuff you are."

Whenever someone suggests that I connect with someone, especially when that person and I share a strong passion, I'm always more than happy to oblige. I enthusiastically asked Andres to put us in touch. My first thought when he said George worked for Tony Robbins was, "Seriously? Is that a good or bad thing?"

Tony Robbins is that big, giant man who, not only had a memorable cameo in *Shallow Hal*, but more notably made millions on self-improvement cassette tapes in the 80s and 90s. Since then, he's written multiple best-selling books around mindset and money and leads massive seminars around the world with hundreds of thousands of his "cult followers" in attendance. This was my perception of Tony Robbins anyway. I watched the Netflix documentary about him called *I'm Not Your Guru* back in 2015 when someone told me my "tough love, matter of fact, not for the faint at heart" coaching style reminded them of his style.

I was intrigued about George's work for Tony's organization because it's almost an impossible job to get. Literally thousands of people apply for his Peak Performance trainer positions each year and only six are hired. George was one of them, so that alone said a lot. When we spoke on the phone, we had an instant connection and love for each other as humans. We geeked out over coaching, mindset, spiritual practices, hardships we had overcome, and those we were currently working through to overcome.

George talked about what he was doing for Tony's organization, and as our call was coming to an end, he unveiled an opportunity. "So, Tony's *Unleash The Power Within* seminar is coming to Dallas next month. I can get you an Executive seat for the General Admission price if you're interested?"

Mind you, Andres and I were still in debt, and my lack mindset was still alive and ugly. Anything over $250 would simply be too much for me to invest in (unless it was a plane ticket for a vacation because my priorities were so out of whack). Plus, I assumed the seminar was thousands of dollars.

Nevertheless, I said, "Tony Robbins is coming to Dallas? I had no idea. What is *Unleash the Power Within*?"

George explained that "UPW" is almost like an entry-level introduction to the self-improvement world of Tony Robbins. When I asked about the cost, he said the general admission ticket was $695 and promised it would be "transformational."

Much like when I stood in the hotel room in Vegas talking to Molly, my ugly lizard brain told me to freeze. And much like when my heart stepped up and took over, it came through again. Something bigger than my brain said, "I must do this. I must invest in myself to get to where I want to be, for the rest of my life." This encounter with George was no coincidence. It was another test.

George and I had to hop off the phone for other calls, but he said he'd call back to get a credit card number. I had time to reconsider. There was time for my brain to get to work on all the reasons why I should not do it. My heart had another agenda. My heart was going to Tony Robbins. Why the hell not?

> This encounter with George was no coincidence. It was another test.

Unleashed

Tony Robbins talks about "juicing" things up. By that, he means making things livelier, more powerful, more attractive, more meaningful, more joyful. I was damn near juice-less before my journey with Molly began. And my juicy-ness still needed some work, despite all she and I had accomplished to date.

The night before *Unleash the Power Within* kicked off, I went to the conference center to register and get my badge. When I entered through the doors that would lead to my supposed transformation, I was guarded and abnormally withdrawn. I'm an extrovert; I don't withdraw.

My brain was on an overdrive of self-talk as I weaved through a path of people high-fiving and rah-rah'ing me as I got closer to the registration desk. With each "You're awesome!" and "WOO HOO! We're so glad you're here!" and "You've got this! High Five!" I internally rolled my eyes. How could anyone be this happy, energized, and almost annoyingly optimistic? What the hell have I gotten myself into? I thought to myself,

"This is going to be a total cheese-fest. No wonder they refer to this as 'the cult!' Everyone here is clearly brainwashed."

On and on my brain balked, trying to make me turn around and run as far away from this place as possible. Surely, this level of enthusiasm was only a tiny sneak peek of the vibe that would be *unleashed* over the next few days when the event actually started. I got my registration packet, begrudgingly high-fived about 50 more people, and went home a little confused, uncertain, and apprehensive to wait for my friend Jessica to arrive.

Jessica and I met in Molly's Cracking Open program. We had an interesting connection through the monthly video webinars we attended. We were fellow badasses, seeking other badassess to encourage, motivate, support, and relate to from where we'd been and where we wanted to go in our life's journey.

The mere process of buying the ticket to *Unleash the Power Within* was almost led by a power outside of my body. Never before had I purposely decided to dive headfirst into what was considered a "life-changing seminar," paid for it with my own money (versus it being something I attended on behalf of an employer), and I planned to go by myself.

Then I got an email from Jessica. She had told Molly that she needed to get away. She didn't want a quiet, yoga, introspection type of experience. She wanted a fiery, in-your-face, take action, ass kicking. Molly told her I was going to Tony's UPW, so she reached out to ask if she could join me.

Ten days later, Jessica showed up on my front porch in Dallas, fresh from Portland, Maine, right after I got home from registering for the event. It was the first time we had ever laid eyes on each other, live and in person. Our first hug lasted for about three minutes. It was instant love. Instant friendship. Instant connection. Instant BFF.

The next morning, we drove to the conference center in Garland, Texas and cautiously, optimistically walked into our first Tony Robbins seminar. As we eyed the people, the crew, the venue, the food options, and acknowledged the loud music coming from inside the arena, we looked at each other and smiled. We were both asking ourselves if we had arrived at a rock concert.

When we opened the door to the arena, the mood was electric. Over 8,000 people of all ethnicities, ages 10—80, from over 60 countries were hugging, high-fiving, chatting, and dancing to the music pumping through the sound system by various behind-the-scenes DJs from Tony's crew. They had all shown up with the same energy, determination, eagerness, and drive to be much better versions of themselves.

So this was "the cult" people speak of? In other words, there wasn't one. Tony has no demographic other than humans who want a more juiced-up life. If that's a cult, I wanted to be a member. Bright-eyed and curious, Jessica and I relaxed into the enthusiasm of the crowd and became a part of the simple demographic. We had shit we wanted to solve in our lives, and we were ready.

When I committed to the seminar, I jumped all in, not really knowing what I was in for. My resolve, resilience, and courage were tested—a few times beyond physical tolerance—in that arena. The larger-than-life Tony Robbins led all 8,000 of us through discussions, lessons, and exercises that would change our lives. Showing up with his huge heart, tough love, and matter of fact approach, we all hung on his every word.

Tony told us exactly what we needed to hear, not what we wanted to hear. Many times, over the next four days, he stressed a "mantra" of sorts: "Never leave the site of a decision before making a commitment to take action." Here I was, absolute about wanting to be at this seminar, already starting to de-clutter the brain and wake the heart up. I was ready to take massive action, and I was #scaredAF.

"Never leave the site of a decision before making a commitment to take action."

He talked us through his "Success Cycle" theory about how beliefs lead to potential that lead to action that lead to results. He taught us the difference between a beautiful state and a suffering state. To be in a beautiful state, we have to change our physiology, our focus, and our language, which Tony trademarked as The Triad™.

There was a powerful presentation about the six basic human needs:

1. Certainty

2. Uncertainty/Variety

3. Significance

4. Connection/Love

5. Growth

6. Contribution

As we worked through this exercise, I realized I'd been searching for certainty and significance versus connection/love most of my life. Uncertainty/variety was the need I avoided the most.

We explored the driving force of momentum, Tony's Pyramid of Mastery, and how disappointment can either drive someone or destroy them. This information caused me pause. I'd been suffering under the control of my own mind for two years. I'd been beating myself up and resentful of others because I was disappointed with where my life was. Disappointment was slowly destroying me. But the moment I decided to work with Molly, and then attend the Tony Robbins seminar, I was experimenting with turning my disappointment from destruction to drive. This realization was one of many aha moments during UPW, but there was still a long way to go.

Disappointment was slowly destroying me.

We discussed what it means to live a fulfilled life and how to be obsessed with appreciation. Tony talked about behaving, thinking, and acting in a way that allows you to be in a peak state. Maintaining a peak state is achieved by giving more than receiving (where had I heard that before?), which creates energy and attracts abundance. Staying in that beautiful state gives you the power and mindset to do anything, like say, walk on fire.

At the end of the first, very long, 13-hour day, Tony took all 8,000 of us out to the parking lot of the conference center. There were rows and rows of fiery coals burning bright red and ready to test our collective and individual mental resolve. This was the famous fire walk, and I was about to find out why. Tony had primed us for how to get in the right state of mind to walk across the fiery coals without getting third-degree burns on our feet.

When my time came to step up and walk across the fire, it was the mental test of all tests. *Look up, don't look down, keep walking, don't stop, and say "cool moss, cool moss, cool moss" the entire way. Ready? Go! COOL MOSS! COOL MOSS! COOL MOSS!* It worked! I felt cool and, without looking down, made it across to the celebratory high fives from loads of strangers as Tony's crew poured water on my feet. I found Jessica, and we jumped up and down and hugged in complete disbelief that we had both, holy shit, walked on fire.

When the energetic high wore off, I started to feel pain on the outside of my right foot. I looked down and there it was, one tiny blistery reminder that said, "Excellent work with the fire walk. I'm here to say that you are still resisting. You have some work to do on surrendering to your fears." Instead of letting the disappointment destroy me, I decided to let it drive me to keep going and unlock whatever was trapped inside.

The Exorcism

On day two, Joseph McClendon III hosted while Tony took a day to rest. I still laugh when I think of one of Joseph's damn near trademarked teachings: "Shake. That. Ass." He taught us to generate positive emotions every morning by shaking our asses to achieve a true ASS-itude. There were a lot of asses shaking in that arena for the next few days!

After two 13-hour days of "reprogramming," I was exhausted and high on energy at the same time. Getting in the groove of how things operated in Tony's world, I was high-fiving anyone and everyone who was even remotely nearby.

Day three was packed solid. Tony was back to walk us through one of his most powerful exercises called the Dickens Process™. This is all about values, beliefs, and eliminating inner conflicts driven by limiting beliefs. At first, he asked his crew to escort any child under the age of 12 out of the arena to one of the designated play areas throughout the convention center. I thought, "Oh shit. What we're about to do is not appropriate for kids? Exactly how scary is this going to get?"

This was one of those turning points in a Tony Robbins seminar where you either hold your nose and jump in or you decide this environment is not for you. I held my nose and jumped.

> ... how scary is this going to get?"

After the children left, Tony had us all write down our limiting beliefs. He instructed us to stand up as the lights went out and his voice boomed across the arena telling us to get limiting belief #1 in our minds. He asked us to reflect on all of the negative outcomes and consequences this one belief had generated.

With everyone focused on their own #1 limiting belief, Tony fired a pile of sobering questions to the crowd: What had we missed out on? What had we not gained? Where would we be five years from now if we held on to this one belief? What about 10 years, 30 years and 50 years? Who would be in our lives and who had we pushed away? Who would we have disappointed and whose love would we have lost? What successes would we have missed out on? What failures were constantly at our feet? We went through the same exercise for all of the limiting beliefs on our lists.

This line of questioning sent me into an almost trance-like state of negativity, but I didn't want to give up. "Out there" though this was, it was unlike anything I'd ever experienced. I realized I was hunched almost all the way over and my head was close to my waist. As I hung there, with the emotional and mental weight of all the past and potential future consequences of my limiting beliefs, I *physically felt* how destructive negative thoughts can be. Later, Jessica said she wanted to check on me but left me alone when she realized I was having a moment.

We all remained standing (or in my case, hunched over) in the dark when Tony's voice changed. It got lighter, and he showed us how to flip the limiting belief. For each old belief, we were to come up with a new, empowering belief. For example, "there will never be enough money" became "money flows in and out and is abundant." As we focused on our new, empowering beliefs, again, my body reacted. I physically shot up, stood tall, boobs out, arms back, and yelled as loud as I could in chorus with thousands of my new seminar friends. It was a sight to see, I'm sure.

Even now, I refer to the experience as a full-on exorcism. Whatever the hell it was, it was the day I cracked open to the next level, fueled by the work I had done up until then with Molly and then having this out-of-body experience at UPW. When I felt actual physical pain as a result of my mental pain, and then found the strength to turn a negative belief into an empowering belief, something in my mindset shifted.

Self-Love Over Logic

Tony's crew does an amazing job supporting the attendees through the UPW experience and all of the emotions that go with it. They also do an amazing job of encouraging people to buy *more* experiences. The intention is to 1) Keep the momentum alive, and 2) Commit to taking the massive action Tony referred to many times.

On the final day of the event, I had a huge decision to make: one that took my anxiety and the push/pull of my heart/brain self-talk to new levels. I wanted more from this journey, and I wanted more for myself.

Initially hesitant about entering Tony's world, I had officially been converted and MASTERY was the path I wanted—a total immersion experience that included three of Tony's life-changing events: *Date With Destiny*, *Life Mastery*, and *Wealth Mastery*. It also included two free tickets to a future UPW event and six months of one-on-one sessions with one of Tony's Results Coaches. All this, for the sarcastically low price of $10,000, which I did not have.

I wanted more from this journey, and I wanted more for myself.

Enter the familiar push and pull of my heart and brain. Since the very first mention of Mastery, my heart screamed yes and my brain screamed no. It went like this, "There is no way. I don't have the money. I'm in debt. But I need it. Hell, I want it. It could be life-changing. Andres will shit a brick. There's no way he'll agree. I'll find a way to make the money. I must do it. Do they offer an interest-free payment plan?"

Queue up Jessica who stepped in to talk me through it. When she asked—"Do you really want *to do* this? For *you*?"—I froze and started crying. That $10K price tag weighed heavily on me and she saw it.

Looking straight into my eyes, she asked, "What just happened? Your entire facial expression, body language, and the color in your face just changed right before me."

I was literally terrified to make the jump with Mastery, strictly from a financial viewpoint. Terr.I.Fied. Matter of fact, I don't recall feeling that conflicted at any other time in my life.

Admitting what she already knew, my internal dialogue came rushing out. "I am terrified. You know I don't have that kind of money. Andres and I have a rule not to spend anything over $1,000 without discussing it. This is 10 times that! I've tried texting and calling but I can't get a hold of him, and I need to decide. Maybe I should start with Tony's recorded courses and apps? I don't know. Let's go ask someone."

We walked over to talk to Zach, a crewmember Jessica had befriended along the way, who was at the counter. He started telling us about *Time*

Of Your Life™, another one of Tony's staple courses. Jessica counted to five before she interrupted him and said to me, "Babe, this is not what you want or need. Mastery is!"

Zach stopped talking, leaned in, and folded his hands under his chin. Jessica grabbed my arm with one hand and pointed at Zach's wrist with the other, "Oh my god. Look!" Hanging from Zach's wrist was a MyIntent bracelet.

MyIntent.org is an amazing service project and mission started by Chris Pan, a friend of Andres' from grad school. It started around the idea of finding your purpose and identifying one word that represents it. The word is hammered into a small, round token and attached to a bracelet or necklace. I happen to be a MyIntent Maker and have made many bracelets for friends, co-workers, and clients over the years.

Jessica said, "Look at his word!" Dangling in front of my face was Zach's intention word: BELIEVE. I looked at her and started crying, heaving actually. Zach came around from the counter and gave me a big hug, and they both slowly and carefully walked me across the floor to the counter for Mastery. It was time to practice what Tony had been preaching: never leave the site of a decision before making a commitment to take action.

It was time to practice what Tony had been preaching.

Literally shaking and crying, I slowly handed over my credit card to someone named Veronica. After she ran the card for an initial down payment of $1,995, she gave me a backpack full of Mastery gear and a huge hug. She looked at me intently and lovingly and said, "No shit Carrie, this will change your life. I tripled my business as a result of Mastery. You cannot and will not see it now but please know, all of the success and happiness you want is coming your way through this journey."

Only time and determination would tell. At that exact moment, I was absolutely scared shitless; not about the journey that was ahead of me, but about when I was going to tell my husband about the decision I had just made.

Find Your Juicy Life

Trust divine timing.
People, places, and things come into our lives when they are meant to. It's up to us to pay attention to the reason they show up and, perhaps, the lesson we are supposed to learn. Trusting things we can't see is sometimes difficult but quite simply, you must trust anyway. Trust that a greater power has your back, and then trust yourself to listen for whatever that greater power sees ahead for you.

Don't let negative self-talk be your guide.
Negative talk has never, and I mean never, helped any of us. As a matter of fact, the asshole that lives in our head is solely focused on keeping us "safe," a.k.a. stuck. Name that voice in your head so you can tell her to shut the hell up, take a hike: she is not welcome here. When you can personify that negative, nagging voice, you can tell that bitch to go away. You can take control of what that voice is telling you.

Follow your intuition.
Have you ever noticed that whenever you do the opposite of what your gut tells you, shit goes off the rails? Always listen to your gut. That's where intuition lives, and it will always guide you down the path of your destiny when you listen to it. We all have the power to get in touch with our intuition. If you are someone who wants to argue with me on that point, then it's time for you to get silent and go meet your intuition. It is there waiting for you. I promise.

Find a guru.
Thank God we live in a society where many, many badasses have gone before us and paved the way to happier everything. Many gurus across several categories are out there willing to share and happy to serve. I just happened to (unexpectedly) find mine in people like Tony Robbins as well as Mel Robbins

(no relation to Tony), and Brené Brown. These three people have shared hard truths that have greatly influenced and inspired me, as well as many others, in different and various ways.

Go explore who resonates with you, follow them on Instagram, listen to their lessons, and absolutely take yourself to a seminar when you are truly ready for massive change.

CHAPTER 7

NAVIGATING REALITY

"Change your decisions and you'll change your life. And what will change your decisions more than anything? Courage."
-Mel Robbins

Infidelity

As anticipated, Andres lost his shit when I told him I'd just signed up for a program that would cost us ten grand. He wasn't mad about me doing Mastery; it was solely about the cost and the timing. Out of town for work, he called me from the road and insisted that I call the Robbins Institute and ask for a refund. He said that I must make the call "first thing in the morning."

Quite simply, I told him I was not going to do that. I had only left the empowering event hours earlier. I was tired, raw, and—in that moment talking to Andres—probably the feistiest I've ever been in our marriage. He kept on, reminding me of our financial situation and asking how I could make such a reckless decision without consulting him. No matter how many times I told him I tried to call, text, and send pictures of the contract without a response on his end, he wasn't having any of it.

I acknowledged what he said, and stubbornly didn't care. It's not lost on me that many people thought (Andres chief among them), and possibly still do, that it was highly irresponsible to add to the debt that we were struggling to pay down. It's hard to explain sometimes. Financially irresponsible? Hell yes! Emotionally and mentally necessary for me? Abso-fucking-lutely.

When you know there is a better life ahead if you take a risk, you take it. This was not a life-or-death type of risk. This was a situation where I wanted a better version of myself, I wanted it now, and Tony's ass kicking environment was what I needed to get there. I knew it to my core. To me, this was not just a *cost*; it was an *investment*. It was worth it to pay interest on my CC to achieve it and find a way to pay for it. I was going all in.

> **When you know there is a better life ahead if you take a risk, you take it.**

Then, Andres proceeded to say something that still stings when I think about it. He yelled loudly on his end of the phone, "You have committed financial infidelity! I am the CFO of our household, and you directly violated our vow of talking before either of us makes a large purchase."

Now, my husband is not a yeller. He's actually the opposite. When he's upset, he usually becomes eerily calm and intentional with his words, which I find scarier. In his tone and his words, I heard his feeling of total betrayal. In this moment, I also heard a raw pain from him, like I had never heard before, and at a volume that was completely out of character for him. In return, he gave that pain right back to me. The last thing I wanted to do was cause my husband and my marriage pain and stress. I also didn't want to stop my journey just as it was getting started, similar to when he was launching his start-up; I went through job after job after job to try to make ends meet financially so he didn't have to stop just as *he* was getting started. The timing of his launch was not ideal either but we forged ahead. He didn't seem to feel the same way about the investment in my journey, primarily the timing of it.

It was a low moment in our amazing marriage. I felt awful for causing him any pain at all, but I refused to back down. My resolve and determination to do what I needed to do for me was firm. We had been investing in his start-up business, we had invested in the kids, and dammit, it was MY fucking turn. My Mastery journey was about me and, in my heart, the timing was now.

> **It was MY fucking turn.**

Our call did not end well but we civilly agreed to talk more about it when he got home the next day. I had already considered calling Tony's world the next morning to discuss a payment plan to ease the pain while remaining persistent about my decided path. Once we hung up, I was shaken, confused, pissed off, sad, and even more determined. There was only one person in the world I wanted to talk to at that moment—my dad.

Mr. Mom Saves the Day

Paul Davis, a.k.a., Mr. Mom, is my dad and knight in shining armor. He's always had my back. After the biggest fight of my marriage, I called him and he mounted his white horse.

My parents separated for a bit when my sister was very little and before I was born. To this day, I joke with my dad that I am totally the result of hot make-up sex. "Dad? Come on, tell me… I know that's why I'm so fiery and passionate!" They stayed friends when the marriage ended, which made joint custody a lot easier and was healthy for us kids.

Kristen and I lived mostly in Austin with Mom and our stepdad, Joe. Dad lived in Dallas with his second wife. We spent almost every other weekend flying Southwest Airlines between the two cities to hang out with Dad. When my mom died in the fall of 1983, Kristen and I finished out the school year with Daddy Joe and moved to Dallas that following June.

We continued to fly Southwest Airlines, in reverse to Austin, to see Daddy Joe who was and always will be a beloved member of the family. A few years after Mom died, he married an incredible human who I call Saint Cathy. She lost her husband to a tragic accident. The Widow and the Widower found each other, and Cathy, along with her three children, gave our stepdad a new lease on life. Thirty-some odd years later, we are all one big, happy, modern family.

After moving in with Dad in Dallas, Kristen and I adjusted to our new town. We were not super close growing up and fought constantly. She's only three and half years older but we were very different. She was always in her room reading and I was always climbing trees. When she went off to college at Texas Tech, there was no tearful farewell. We were all, "Bye! Whatever."

A few years later, she came to visit me one weekend when I was at UT Austin, and there was a shift in our relationship. We were completely caught off guard and totally confused by how cool and fun the other sister was. Under this new light, our sisterhood blossomed. She would become my best friend, the most incredible aunt, and one of my biggest supporters.

We finish each other's sentences, love long car drives together where we can sing to Yacht Rock at the top of our lungs, and if we get going with laughter, eventually there is no sound coming out of our open mouths. With eyes clinched, and tears streaming down our faces, we buckle over trying to catch our breath until the volume of the laughter returns. It's the best feeling in the world. She is my fiercely protective mama bear. Even though we are still very different, our relationship is iron clad with love.

Despite the ambivalence of our younger years, Kristen and I called each other "Noni." The pet name came from a random joke one of her ex-boyfriends made a million years ago and, for some hilarious reason, it stuck.

Over the years, Noni, Dad, and I became a united force to be reckoned with. The Three Musketeers, as we call ourselves, have ridden many waves of loss, love, travel, school adventures, laughter, and kids—Lucas and Lala and Noni's daughter, Sydney. No matter what, we Three Musketeers will always have each other and our inside jokes. Our respective families and friends know not to interfere with the dynamic.

Whenever Kristen or I have been in trouble—emotionally, mentally, physically, or financially—Dad is always the first to arrive and save the day. Before I called him to discuss the Tony Robbins Mastery fiasco I caused in my marriage, I took a deep breath and thought through what I wanted to say to him. I needed his ear and knew he would jump in.

My push-pull was at it again. Mentally, I hoped Dad would help ease the financial pain and loan me the money. Emotionally, I felt guilty for even thinking about asking. My pride was pissed because I'd already borrowed thousands of dollars when we were dealing with our housing crunch problem. Though I'd paid back every penny, I couldn't believe I needed his help again. I called him, and we dove into it.

My dad thinks Andres is a great guy, and they get along well. But of course, he's still my dad, so don't fuck with his daughter! I knew he'd do whatever it took to calm me down and wipe away my tears.

Dad is fair, if not generous. He is always there to ease the pain for both Kristen and me and is adamant about it being balanced. We've always talked about how he is essentially the de facto Chairman of the Board for my business. He gave me the money to purchase CareerFrame.com when I first launched (because unfortunately, it was not one of those $12 URLs on GoDaddy.com). Now, we were talking about $10,000 for investment into my personal growth. Of course, he told me to take the money out of his account and not to worry about it. I was part relieved and part reluctant to borrow the money. He insisted, and so I stopped resisting and gratefully accepted the life raft.

Still adamant that I get a refund for my purchase (which at the time was only a $1,995 deposit), Andres likely thought it was pathetic that I went crawling to Daddy. I thought it was determined. I wanted this path, and I found a way to get it. Whereas I wanted my husband's blessing and encouragement, not getting either was not going to slow me down. I wasn't asking for his permission; I was granting it to myself unapologetically.

Dark Night of the Soul

After UPW, I stopped taking my anti-anxiety medication cold turkey. Although I knew that it was a bad idea to quit a mind-altering chemical abruptly, my reasoning seemed rational at the time. My concern was that the meds were suppressing some emotions that really needed to come out. I thought, "I conquered my deepest fears at UPW and through my work with Molly. Surely, I can conquer Wellbutrin."

I could not. I absolutely fell apart, and the anxiety returned in full force. With it came an amazing dose of daily crying, sometimes for no reason at all. One night, I was soaking and sobbing in the bathtub, aware of my depression and anxiety, and missing my mother badly. Yet, it felt as though something was being shed or released.

The next day, when I described the sensation to Molly, she said, "Oh honey! You're going through the dark night of the soul!"

I said, "The dark night of the who-zee-whats-it?"

She laughed and repeated the phrase, "The dark night of the soul. It's a period in your life when you're going through something difficult and painful—like a death, or a breakup, or facing your own mortality. I think you are experiencing death: the death of the old you. You are officially cracking open, letting the light in. The 'you' that is codependent on suffering is dying."

Oh.

> An old, raggedy, decaying, lifeless, negative part of me was gasping her last breaths.

As Molly described this process to me, I had to acknowledge that I did feel like a part of me was dying. An old, raggedy, decaying, lifeless, negative part of me was gasping her last breaths so a brighter, happier, purpose-driven Carrie could be born.

Molly said, "Keep going, honey! Keep going. Keep crying and let that old part of you go. Find the beauty in the pain and go through it all. Don't brush it away."

As she suggested, I continued to sit through that dark night of the soul and told Andres to let me keep crying. If it lasted too long, I promised, we could talk through what to do about it. Wellbutrin withdrawal or not, a break from the medication helped make space to get the gunk out. After the eight-month grief party over my mom and the powerful experience at UPW, my soul was waking up, and I was excited to finally meet her.

A few days later, and having moved on from the major disagreement in our marriage about Mastery, Andres sat me down on the couch for a talk. Not usually a fan of medication, it was he who suggested I go back on the meds. He supported the catharsis, but the reality was that I was a rookie when it came to managing my anxiety without medication (or wine). As much as I was empowered by what I'd learned through Tony and what I was working through with Molly, the crying was at an unhealthy level, especially with my kids running around to see it. To be clear, I was not afraid to cry in front of my kids, but the frequency was not ideal. Reluctantly, I agreed with Andres and got back on the meds because brain chemistry is real. And within two weeks, the crying ceased to a dull roar and we could see the medication really did help.

Brain chemistry is real.

Boot on the Ass

The heavy, unfulfilled feeling related to my corporate job was just as real and impossible to ignore as my brain chemistry. Andres saw how hard I was trying to get to CareerFrame Island and gave me a challenge. He basically coached me like I coach others and said, "If you're serious about this, do something about it. Set a departure date 60 to 90 days out from now and start networking to find clients. I support you, Babe."

Challenge accepted. I gave myself 75 days to leave corporate and go back to my coaching business. 75 days sounded reasonable. Until it wasn't.

As the weeks ticked by, the saboteur inside my brain made an appearance in a grandiose way. I felt overly confident with my deadline but lacked the courage to take real or meaningful action. My networking efforts were half-assed while my negative self-talk worked triple overtime. It was like two steps forward with Tony and Molly, and one giant leap backwards with the inner critic.

In assessing my behavioral patterns, something important dawned on me. When I hired Molly initially, I committed to 12 months. My intuition told me we would unearth some things at three months, hopefully see some shifts by month six and by month nine, I predicted shit would get real, and hard, and I'd want to give up. And here I was. At the nine-month mark, on the verge of stepping across the line to take control over my life and career happiness, and I was coming up with every reason to sabotage it so I would have something to blame, something to lose, and something to confirm my biggest fear.

To her immense credit, Molly wasn't having it. She put the verbal boot on my ass and helped push me through the destructive self-talk that was clouding my judgment. My cocky self loved the end date I'd set for the corporate job. My intuitive self said to hang in a bit longer and get properly prepared.

Molly helped me sift through my ego, confusion, and desires to see that the 75-day challenge was not quite working as intended. Not only was it a bit premature but I would also miss out on a little pile of cha ching. There was the strong potential for a nice end-of-year bonus from corporate; if I left by the 75-day date, I'd be leaving that pile of money on the table. And the truth was, we needed that money as much as I needed to get back to CareerFrame. The amount was worth the short-term un-fulfillment.

I made the decision to stick it out for a few more months, which gave me the opportunity to complete my journey with Molly. So, challenge delayed due to reality.

Find Your Juicy Life

Vows are not meant to be broken.
I will never encourage someone to break a vow (any vow) with a loved one. It causes too much pain, it breaks trust, and it's simply not okay. At the same time, I might argue that there are very rare occasions when a vow needs to be slightly bent, as in my situation. If you have a solid, steady, unshakeable relationship, I can argue that bending may be necessary to unapologetically put yourself first, especially if you can actually SEE the path to get through the misalignment with the other person and that your decision is not ultimately going to do massive harm. For example, the only reason I bent the financial vow in my marriage was because I knew I would find a way to relieve the "short-term" financial pain and because I knew that ultimately, Andres and I would both come out stronger through my journey. In a strong relationship, the bend will repair; so think through the consequences and act as you need to. Bold advice, I know.

Find a way.
It took me a year to get the word "can't" out of my vocabulary. Other than rising from the dead, there is almost nothing we "can't" do. When you know you need to do something, then you must do it, especially if it's FOR YOU: find a way. You are not allowed to physically harm yourself or someone else to find a way. You find a way emotionally, financially (which does not include stealing and the like), spiritually, and mentally in order to keep yourself on the track you know you are meant to be on.

Keep going.
When shit gets hard, the perfect environment for giving up is created. Please don't. This is when courage will make an incredible appearance if you ask for it. Find someone to put a boot on your ass and help you be accountable when the tough gets going. You have the courage to do anything your heart desires. Listen and take action.

CHAPTER 8

BREAKTHROUGH

"Frustration means you are about to have a breakthrough."
-*Tony Robbins*

Show Yourself

Lala, who has always been the sparkling light in our family, is a big fan of Disney's movie *Frozen*. (Truth be told, I'm a pretty big *Frozen* fan myself.) When *Frozen 2* came out, she was ecstatic to see Elsa again. I took her on a special mommy/daughter date to the movies, a huge tub of popcorn nestled between us, our eyes glued to the screen expectantly.

Spoiler Alert: toward the end of the movie, Elsa follows a mysterious voice that has been singing to her from afar. When she reaches Ahtohallan, the glacial river of memory, she begins singing the now famous song, "Show Yourself." As she enters a giant cavern, she discovers the origin of the voice that has been calling to her. The ghost of Elsa's mother, who was killed in a shipwreck many years earlier, is there and together, they burst into harmony for the chorus of the song.

Show yourself

Step into the power

Grow yourself

Into something new

Then, Elsa's mom sings: *You are the one you've been waiting for*, and Elsa follows with: *All of my life; All of your life. Oh, show yourself.* In that moment, it is revealed that Elsa's mother is the source of her daughter's magical powers, and it is Elsa's destiny to step into those powers.

As I watched the scene unfold, sitting next to my 6-year-old daughter in the dark, the lyrics of the song penetrated my soul. With heaving shoulders, tears began to pour down my face. Trying to conceal my emotional outpouring from Lala, so as not to cause her to worry, I reflected on the immense growth I'd experienced on my journey with Molly. This was shortly after she had put her verbal boot on my ass, and the vast majority of my healing had been centered on grieving the loss of my mom. Now, it was as if MY mother was sending me a message through Elsa and her mother's song in *Frozen 2*. I felt her around me and, as I cried in the cocoon of the dark movie theater, I thought, "I hear you, Mom. You're telling me that I am the one I've been waiting for. It's time to step into my power, and I'm not going to let either of us down."

For the next month, I listened to "Show Yourself" almost daily, and couldn't hear it without crying. It was not gentle crying either; it was the breakdown type of crying. The song reinforced my resistance to step into my own power. It put a spotlight on my fear to take the leap despite the growing desire to do so.

During my last phone session with Molly in December, I heard the song playing from another room. Lala told Alexa to play it, as we both often did that winter. I immediately started crying and asked Molly, "Why can't I hear this song without crying? Why am I resisting?"

She calmly said, "Lean into the fear, Sweetie. Let it be your guide. It's time. You're ready."

She was right. I was.

Lean into the fear. Let it be your guide.

A Date with Destiny

As my journey with Molly wrapped up, it was time to go all in with Mastery. My Tony Robbins soul sister, Jessica (who also had decided on Mastery), and I met up in West Palm Beach, Florida to attend the much anticipated, first seminar of the Mastery series, *Date With Destiny*. DWD is Tony's favorite annual gathering, and he leads it with passion for six straight 13-hour days. Thrilled to reunite on this transformational path, Jessica and I were pumped up and ready for whatever this next phase of our juiced-up learning would entail.

True to Tony's signature style, we kicked off day one with rock concert energy and enthusiasm, just as we had at *Unleash the Power Within*. The big man himself spoke to the crowd about insatiable hunger, which is a precursor for massive growth. He shared stories of empowering mindset shifts around the most powerful of all human forces: emotions. He introduced emotions within the context of the three masteries of life: cognitive, emotional and physical. For example: you understand something, you feel it, and then you do something with it. Life tosses problems at us daily but they are actually gifts because they propel us to act and grow, which is a sign of life. He explained that problems need energy to survive and yet, resistance to changing the "software" of our minds is exactly what keeps us stuck.

During this discussion, it felt like Tony was speaking to me directly. I was the capital Q, Queen of Resistance. I held on to all of my pain with a death grip because it was familiar; I was comfortable sitting in it. But I had to admit that my quality of life was determined by the emotions associated with every aspect of that pain, good and bad. My notes from day one are peppered with phrases like: Joy is missing. Slow down and embrace joy. One of my notes literally says: Stop fucking sabotaging the ability to see and feel joy that is all around me now! Whoa.

Stop fucking sabotaging the ability to see and feel joy.

On day two, all of the attendees were broken out into smaller groups. Jessica and I went our separate ways and planned to reconnect on breaks to share stories and experiences. Within the groups, we were prepped to identify our Primary Question[1], which is described as the dominant question that permeates your conscious and unconscious thinking. It becomes the ultimate laser and/or filter for what you consistently notice (or fail to notice) and experience in your life. Typically, it's a survival instinct question, with built-in beliefs about the consequences, and one that embodies your identity.

My primary question, for as long as I could remember, was: "When am I going to lose what I have?" Because my ultimate fear was loss, this question was my lens for almost everything. This was a powerful moment of clarity. Through my work with Molly and my new experiences in Tony's world, I learned that anything we say after the words "I am" is what we are inviting into our lives. My internal dialogue said: "I am not worthy"; "I am sad"; "I am anxious about losing a loved one"; "I am in debt." (And so on, and so on.) I had been inviting loss—instead of joy or abundance—into my life simply by the language I used in my subconscious Primary Question.

Realization in hand, I crafted a new Primary Question aimed towards the immediacy of the moment as well as the feelings and emotions I was seeking. The result was: How can I experience faith, trust, joy and grace in my life *now*?

Day three is often when people have a breakthrough at a Tony event. They're so tired, exhausted, and emotionally raw that they are primed for the breakdown to allow new beliefs to come through. Despite some aha moments, I hadn't had any major breakthroughs yet and as exhausted as I was, I was indeed primed.

While at the event, I tried to mentally disconnect from life at home, especially work, to focus on the growth path in front of me. Despite my efforts, a huge distraction came barreling into my headspace that had to be addressed.

[1] https://www.tonyrobbins.com/living-primary-question/

An employee on my team was out on vacation. In their absence, a disgruntled client started to vocalize displeasure with some things my employee had done, or more accurately, not done. While they were away, we had another amazing employee, who I call The Fixer, covering their work correspondence. Whenever The Fixer stepped in on any client issue, it was always resolved beautifully. Then, I would sit back and anticipate the client's request that The Fixer be appointed their new account manager. The Fixer was that good (and still is).

With this particular disgruntled client, even The Fixer was baffled as to how to resolve the issue. Knowing I was immersed in a personal experience in Florida, they were racked with guilt for having to loop me in on emails or text me questions, which then led *me to feel guilty* if I didn't check email or respond to their texts immediately. Because I cared about The Fixer and appreciated them greatly, it was easy for me to support them from the event, even if it was an inconvenience.

My frustration and distraction over the disgruntled client grew throughout the day as the correspondence back and forth continued. My frustration wasn't aimed at The Fixer; they were trying to fix an unpleasant situation. My frustration was with the entire situation of wondering why I was perceived to be the only person at my corporate job who could help with this. I had peers and leadership who, at the time, I also perceived were not willing or able to cover for me, knowing I was attending this very important event. Part of me totally understood that no matter where I was, the work and clients were my responsibility as the leader of my team, but the majority of me was simply mad about it all.

At one point, I had to get up and leave the arena to take a call with the client and ensure all was smoothed over. The call took me out of Tony's empowering mindset and thrust me into a mental atmosphere of pure annoyance and aggravation.

Irritations such as this one only reinforced my yearlong desire to leave corporate and grow my own business. That desire grew stronger as I paced *outside* of the arena on my phone, painfully aware of the precious minutes I was missing *inside* that would propel me closer to my goal. When I finally hung up, I changed my focus for a moment to the future.

The story I had been telling myself was that I needed at least one committed, long-term client of my own to make the jump. There was a media company I'd been courting for over a year but they had been uncertain of their plans and seemed apprehensive about pulling the trigger. I had a proposal in front of them after the yearlong back and forth and was focused on bringing it to fruition. They wanted to talk while I was at my seminar and, unlike the corporate phone call, this was a call I wanted to take. My mind was hanging on the potential that this was the engagement I'd been hungering for—could this be the opportunity to leap from corporate into CareerFrame full time? They'd been slow moving in the past. Could I reasonably expect a commitment from them this time?

The media company and I hopped on a call as I paced in anticipation of exciting news. The situation unfolded as such—they were interested, they were appreciative of my patience, and they still had pause on the logistics. They wanted me to attend a meeting two months from then to see how things went, if I was a fit, and then they would like more discussion on a decision. It was something, but it wasn't the slam-dunk I hoped for. To them, I kept an optimistic attitude as we finished our call. When I hung up, I was far from being in a peak state and, filled with uncertainty, I slumped back into the arena.

When I got back to my seat, my brain kicked in. The media company, their apprehension, and its potential for CareerFrame took a mental place on the left side of my mind. *Date with Destiny* and all that it stirred up was on the right side. The corporate job was front and center, and I mentally stared daggers of fire directly at it. The gratitude I had for the lifeboat hit the pause button big time.

The Pivotal Moment

Sitting there in my seat, I tuned Tony's booming voice out as tunnel vision kicked in. My heart started racing. My breathing got shorter as my frustration grew rapidly. Anger reared its head. Longing for CareerFrame magnified. The media company's uncertainty taunted me. And to create the absolutely perfect conditions for me to lose my shit, disdain for my current position with the corporate job grabbed hands with fear. All the feelings combined in order to crash through the doors of my mind and head straight for my heart, and I went into a full-blown panic attack.

As tears gushed down my face and I struggled to breathe, the girl next to me asked how she could help. Shaking like a leaf, I excused myself and ran to the lobby. A team leader approached to ask if I was okay. Barely able to talk, I responded louder than necessary with a decisive NO! She then asked if she could hug me, to which I responded by throwing my arms around her before she changed her mind. Clutching onto her for dear life, she steered me outside. When the sunlight hit my face, I started shaking my head, hands and arms in an attempt to shake off the feelings that were overwhelming me.

The team leader walked me in a large circle around the courtyard of the convention center as she talked me through the panic. She helped me catch my breath and get centered on what caused the attack. I told her about the client call, the call with the media company, and about my growing desire to leave my corporate job and go back to my coaching business while feeling fearful. The money panic from UPW was there too, and it felt heavy. It was torturing me that I felt so stuck. Yet, something was different. As the team leader kept me walking and breathing, I found myself starting to shift.

All of the sudden, and amidst the emotional overwhelm, I could feel that I was starting to create space for hope and possibility. I remembered the words on a massive banner hanging in the arena I'd seen the day before. It said, "Frustration means you are about to have a breakthrough." Here I was, beyond frustrated at my ongoing situation but as that banner came into my mind, I started to embody its message. I started to calm down, and I let myself feel my emotions through a slightly different lens.

Slowly, I turned to the team leader and said, "I think I'm having a breakthrough! I know what I must do. Tony tells us to never leave the site of a decision before making a commitment to take action. I'm going to leave the corporate company—no matter what. I do not have the energy to give them anymore. I am making an exit plan, and I'm done."

That moment at *Date With Destiny* was the critical tipping point that sealed the course for my journey to a juicy life. Many of us can vividly recall where we were, what we were wearing, and what surrounded us when we made a pivotal, life-impacting decision. That will forever be the moment I recall when my life took a hard, sharp turn towards a happier life by choosing to make a bold decision for myself. The next steps were suddenly crystal clear. I was able to get myself together, honor my emotions, and wrap it all up with some form of an action plan. I had to laugh a little when I recalled that banner: "Frustration means you are about to have a breakthrough." Well, I'll say!

The Warrior, The Magician and The Vault

The next morning, I was exhausted but positively anxious to see what day four would bring. Jessica and I returned to the arena, found our groups, and settled in for whatever would come next.

As usual, Tony did not disappoint. He walked us through Carl Jung's Four Primary Archetypes: the Warrior, the Magician, the Lover and the Sovereign. He explained how each archetype is connected to the gateway emotions of anger, fear, grief and joy and they impact how we make our decisions in life. Then, he asked us to identify where each of these archetypes lived in our bodies. This brought new meaning to me about how the body communicates with us, and it gave names to the voices in my head. Thinking about having four personas inside your body helps you make decisions from differing viewpoints, without sounding or feeling like a crazy person.

The warrior focuses on mastery of the physical, and her gateway emotion is anger. She faces great challenges head on, dares where others recoil, and willingly steps out of her comfort zone. She fights evil and sacrifices herself for a worthy cause. As Tony's voice boomed at us, my hands searched for where the warrior lived inside me. They hovered over my heart, which didn't feel right but I kept them there.

The magician is the master of transformation, and her gateway emotion is fear. She has a way of gaining insight into the great mystery of the universe through wisdom and intuition. She teaches, designs, constructs, heals and is able to turn wounds into gold. My hands remained over my heart but this time with more conviction. My magician was telling my warrior she was in the wrong place, and I felt it. With absolute clarity, I knew that my magician lived in my heart and my warrior was now without a home. My hands then went to my gut, and instantly, I thought, "HELLO! My warrior lives in my gut."

As I contemplated the physical homes inside my body of these two archetypes, it made sense. My warrior was born when my mom got sick. I always wanted to protect her and, yes, that was from a place in the heart. No wonder I was confused at first as to where my warrior belonged. After my mom died, my warrior moved into protection mode of *my* heart, filled with fierce anger about her loss, and primarily from a place of survival and gut instinct.

When I found my magician, who was quite content in the heart, it felt almost like a little palpitation. She too had been protecting my heart but through the emotion of fear. She was the reason that I was scared to love too deeply, for fear I would lose the love again, as I had when my mom died. My magician had a little dark side, and I imagined her looking at me like a sly fox with the playful, evil smile and raised eyebrows. This vision stirred something within me.

In my mind, I imagined psychologically that the magician and the warrior worked together to put my heart in a vault, and sealed it up inside another vault, protected from feeling any more pain and fueled by anger and fear. That visualization of the sly look on the magician's face told me that perhaps it was time to unlock the vaults, calm the anger, and lean into the fear.

Perhaps it was time to unlock the vaults, calm the anger, and lean into the fear.

For the first time in literally decades, I wanted my heart to play freely yet cautiously. It was the same feeling as wanting to let my kids ride their bikes around the neighborhood without being afraid they would get kidnapped.

I stood with my hands on my heart and visualized the magician opening up the vault. Out came a rose gold-colored sparkly heart that zipped and danced around, full of happiness, and then it went back into the vault. Clearly, I still had some work to do.

Next, Tony moved on to discuss the lover, who focuses on sensuality, sexuality, dance, song, flow, softness, vulnerability and openness. Her gateway emotion is grief. This one was easy. My fingers immediately went to my lips because I am a kisser. Kissing friends and family, especially my husband and children, and anyone I love has always brought me peace and happiness; it is the antidote to the grief I carried through the decades. Next!

The last archetype, and the grandest, was the sovereign. She has a genuine wish for the happiness of others and helps them to see their inherent worth. Her gateway emotion is joy. She bestows that joy by giving blessings, demonstrating compassion, exuding tolerance, and bestowing vision and harmony through psychological cohesion. I paused as Tony's voiced boomed. This one was important. I wanted the sovereign to lead, and I imagined her as peaceful yet strong, calm, decisive, and focused. In the spirit of changing the self-talk track that had been playing for decades, I slowly placed my hands on my shoulders where I carried stress. I wanted the sovereign to live there now so she could address the challenges that lay ahead. I wanted her to bring the joy that was at the center of my new Primary Question.

This powerful exercise opened my eyes and heart to the emotions that had been guiding me my entire life. Shedding the anger, fear, and grief made way for the joy I craved. I consciously would not let any of my archetypes live in my head. As Tony says, "In the head, you're dead. In the heart, you're smart." My mind had me trapped for so long, and I was now focused on making decisions for the future from the other two brains in my body: my gut and my heart. The lips and shoulders would follow. Through this, I started to feel hope and possibility growing inside my heart, and felt certain that everything was going to be okay. I didn't know how, but I was confident that because I had my why, I would find a way. And in that moment, I was at peace.

As Tony says, "In the head, you're dead. In the heart, you're smart."

Toward the Dream

By day five, we were all buzzing, high on energy from what we had already experienced and learned. As a busy working mom who was working through a personal transformation, the first lesson of the day smacked me across the face.

We were told to write a list of what we desired with the mentality that they would also be real goals. I was a champ at to-do lists and a pro at being efficient with my calendar! Constantly on the go with work, shuttling the kids around, and managing the household, I kept lists and calendar entries of everything that needed to be accomplished on a daily basis. From that perspective, I quickly wrote down 27 goals. While I looked down proudly at my list, the big man himself said if we had written down more than five things, it was too much. You don't have to be a rocket scientist, or a brilliant mom, to know that 27 goals is whack-a-doodle.

I worked hard to dwindle my list down to five and then prioritized them:

Love myself (body, mind, and spirit)

Love my spouse

Love my kids

Love my customers

Love others

I told myself that when these goals were accomplished on a daily basis, I could make room for other goals from the original list.

Identifying goals was followed by an awesome, inspiring overview of *Business Mastery*, another one of Tony's favorite seminars. Some of the world's greatest business minds have benefitted from *Business Mastery*. In fact, Marc Benioff, the founder and CEO of Salesforce.com, birthed his business plan for the company during the seminar decades ago. He is now a frequent speaker at *Business Mastery* along with other greats like Sara Blakely, the founder of Spanx.

We revisited the necessity for insatiable hunger, discussed the psychology of a business owner and the CEO mindset—own it, don't run it—and talked about specific strategies such as building a business map, constant innovation and optimization, marketing, numbers, and how to create raving fans. I took pages of notes to lay the groundwork for the future success of CareerFrame.

Tony introduced the importance of being aware of masculine and feminine energy and how it impacts relationships in our professional and personal lives. Every human being, born male or female, has both masculine and feminine energy. Masculine energy is strong and stable. It shows up as self-confidence and decisiveness. It knows what it wants and goes after it, with direction and purpose. Feminine energy is about creative expression, dancing, playing, being internal, and allowing others to nurture you, as you nurture them.

Opposites attract, so when someone with masculine energy meets someone with feminine energy, sparks fly. When two people show up with the same energy, the "sameness" sparks a collision. This perspective and knowledge made me think about how Andres and I can get snippy when we both display masculine energy aimed in different directions. We each have the tendency to be decisive from our own perspectives. When one of us allows the other to take the lead, we are close and loving with each other. I couldn't wait to hug him and explore this dynamic together. But it would have to wait; *Date with Destiny* was about to come full circle back to reframing our Primary Question.

I thought about, "How can I experience faith, trust, joy and grace in my life now?" as Tony prompted us to explore the values and emotions that led us "away" from the question and the values and emotions that led us "toward" it. Through this exercise, I realized that we really do have to look internally for our destiny versus relying on external factors we cannot control. Yet, external factors are the key drivers for the emotions we assign to our feelings.

How can I experience faith, trust, joy and grace in my life now?

My "away" values were clear to me by this point: fear, anxiety, anger, doubt, and at the top of the list, sadness. I would do almost anything to avoid feeling sad. Thankfully, my "toward" values list was much longer and more encouraging: love, connection, abundance, appreciation, playfulness, flow, truth, joy, integrity, inspiration, contribution, courage, honor, and topping the list was the value of experience. Through experiences, I would feel all the other "toward" values on the list.

Next, we were instructed to establish rules around both sets of values. I regularly refer back to this assignment because of how deeply it resonated for me.

My "toward" rules:

I experience **Experiences** anytime I learn or see something new, feel a new emotion, and find warmth and familiarity.

I experience **Love and Connection** anytime I feel nurtured, lovingly touched, understood, heard, seen, and when truth is present.

I experience **Abundance** anytime I have pure joy, give or receive lots of kisses, have financial security, happiness, and a healthy family.

I experience **Appreciation** anytime I stop and think about gifts: material, mental, physical, or emotional, as well as have opportunities for growth and contribution.

I experience **Playfulness** and **Flow** anytime I let myself go and truly enjoy the beauty in the moment.

For the "away" rules, I also created a solution to reframe the emotion that took me away from living my best life.

I will experience **Sadness** only if I think painful loss is the only outcome.

Solution: accept that when something ends, something new begins; when something dies, something is born; when something is lost, something is found.

I will experience **Fear** only if I consistently assume that fear leads to a negative outcome.

Solution: use fear to guide and challenge myself towards rewarding outcomes and overall growth.

I will experience **Anxiety** only when I let external forces control my outcome.

Solution: bring the situation back to what I can control and trust the outcomes of things I can't.

I will experience **Anger** only if I feel strongly about being wronged or accused of something I did not do.

Solution: seek to understand the true meaning behind accusations and show compassion while trusting the lessons in the outcomes.

I will experience **Doubt** only if I allow self-talk to lead me down a dead end, irrational rabbit hole

Solution: find a productive mental ladder and climb out of the rabbit hole.

Because I was striving to get back to CareerFrame, which is centered on helping people reframe their careers, this exercise moved mountains in terms of my own growth. The power of reframing our beliefs and values was not lost on me.

The final giant takeaway from *Date with Destiny* was to create our own personal mission statement. With clarity around my Primary Question, my archetypes happily assigned to their respective homes, and a deeper understanding of my "toward" values, my mission flowed out easily.

"The purpose of my life is to generate connections, enjoy all experiences, serve and be the hero to myself and to others."

The purpose of my life is to generate connections, enjoy all experiences, serve and be the hero to myself and to others.

I was ready to put my dream into motion. *Date with Destiny* gave me the tools and confidence to set a course for CareerFrame Island. What had once seemed so far off in the distance was now coming into view. The corporate job was simply a means to an end, and the end was near. I had given what I could to the corporate job and greatly appreciated all that it gave me in my lifeboat when I needed it. But now with the end in sight, I couldn't wait for what this ending would begin.

Find Your Juicy Life

Attend a life-changing seminar.
Outside of doing the work yourself, the best way to get to where you want to be is to identify someone who is already there, mirror what they have done to the best of your ability, and let their actions and wisdom guide you. Seminars are a great addition to any transformational journey because when you immerse yourself in a mindset that creates shifts; the shifts will actually start to occur. Tony Robbins catapulted me forward to unapologetically claim my juicy life.

Assess your "toward" and "away" values.
To break patterns, we have to be mindful of the stories we've been telling ourselves. What emotions are taking you away from living your best, juicy life and what emotions help you get closer to claiming it? Like the exercise I shared, identify those emotions and reframe them for a solution to keep you focused on your ideal outcome. Pain is an amazing teacher. Show up for the lesson; it will be worth it.

Reflect on pivotal moments.
Remembering pivotal moments that influenced you to take action is an inspiring way to self-coach when other decision points cross your life path. Once you take massive action in your life, you cannot un-see the strength you used to take it and therefore, you can do it again. I won't believe that someone has NEVER had a pivotal moment where they made a decision that impacted their life—for better or worse. Today is always a great day to either reflect on not-awesome decisions you can't un-see and make a massive change in the other direction, or reflect on when you made a kick ass decision that catapulted you towards happiness, and do it again!

Lessons Learned through F.E.A.R.

(Find. Everything. And. Rise.)

From my very first coaching session with Molly, she helped me realize that transformation doesn't happen overnight. I wanted her to "fix" me quickly so I could hurry up and get back to my coaching business. But fixing takes time, which is not easy for someone (me) who has lived life at breakneck speed. Slowing down was really hard and also completely necessary. Slowing down was the first step to finding fulfillment and being able to go all in.

When I was determined to set my sights on a future outcome, there was work to do to reach it. I had to trust myself and I had to trust Molly as my guide. I learned that even though money was super top of mind for me, if I simply followed the dollar signs, or said "no" to opportunities because of dollar signs, things could have gone very badly.

I learned that our true fear is deeper than we may think and it often fuels the surface level fears. I had been telling myself a story about what my true fear was at my core. When I knew what to call my fear, I could then start to focus on healing it. I started telling myself that when something is lost, something else will be found.

Changing decades of behaviors, patterns, and limiting beliefs takes awareness and active, conscious practice. It also takes a shitload of courage. I learned that I had that courage, even in the face of fear. When I allowed myself to think differently, I realized that fear was my guide, not a deterrent. I learned that I could do hard things that seemed painful because I was able to see and feel that something better, whatever it was, was waiting for me to claim it.

We have to give ourselves grace and allow space for necessary change so we can claim our juicy life and share it with others. I learned to reframe frustration. Now when I'm frustrated, I actually get excited that something huge is about to present itself that could quite possibly land me in a place of eureka! The language we use and what we focus on truly, directly impacts our life path. The more I was negative, the more I got negativity in return. The more I chose courage and leaned in, the more positive outcomes came my way. Learning to call out the lizard brain whenever it started yapping was a major growth area for me and has served me well.

Having my coach, being introduced to the world of Tony Robbins, allowing myself to grieve, to grow, and to show myself that I was ready for the next phase of my life set me up for Carrie 2.0. All the work primed me for what I was to accomplish and attract. It was worth every tear, every smile, every panic attack, every frustration, and every triumph. And the best part, my husband saw the change, my kids felt it, my friends and family noticed it, and my clients benefitted. I will forever look at 2019 as the year that changed my life and when I chose to claim my power.

PART 3
FULFILLED

CHAPTER 9

NO MATTER WHAT

"Whether you think you can or think you can't, you're right!"
-Henry Ford

Certifiable

After another life-changing event and massive breakthrough, my heart was singing for CareerFrame and it was time to listen. No matter what—as I told the team leader at *Date with Destiny*. Nothing would take my eyes off the horizon this time.

With Andres' full support, which I greatly appreciated, I thought through the timing of my impending resignation. The potential bonus from corporate was still a strong possibility, and I was still in talks with the media company. The official invite to their annual retreat, and the opportunity to show them that I was a fit for their culture, was in movement and on my calendar. It was essentially a trial run to determine if they wanted to engage with me for the rest of the year and I was ready to show them the value I would bring for the rest of 2020 and beyond.

As planning for the next phase of CareerFrame continued, a friend reached out via text to gauge my interest in a potential lead she had for me. A company in Virginia wanted to do a strengths-based team building exercise. I responded enthusiastically, "Hell, yes, I'm interested!" And then stopped in my tracks when she typed out, "Are you CliftonStrengths® certified?"

There it was, in black and white, the question I had managed to avoid for years. I had put off getting certified because, up until that point, I didn't think I needed it. I was self-taught in Gallup's CliftonStrengths® through listening to Gallup podcasts, taking formalized notes, and even building a study binder. I had attended the Gallup Coach's Summit in Omaha, Nebraska twice and worked with other strengths coaches to ensure I deeply understood the methodologies around the assessment.

My knowledge of how the tool worked grew simply by using it. Practice makes perfect, as they say, and up until my friend posed this question, I had practiced with hundreds of people through various one-offs and my previous gig with the toy company explaining strengths dynamics successfully and effectively. I told myself that if someone was hell bent on me being officially certified, then I guess they wouldn't hire me. Hello, ego. Not being certified was never an issue, until now.

My friend's question made me pause and quickly assess. The media company I'd been wooing was also a CliftonStrengths® culture and having my official certification would only solidify my expertise on the methodology. I started to think that this question was probably going to keep coming up. If I was really serious about CareerFrame this time, having official certifications would only help me and my clients by having proof that I did, in fact, know what I was talking about.

At that moment, I didn't want to risk this, and potential future opportunities, by saying, "No, as a matter of fact, I'm not certified." Despite not wanting to spend the high four-figure cost for certification on content I already knew very well, I couldn't afford to lose out on a technicality. This was a critical stepping-stone along the CareerFrame path, and it was simply the responsible and smart thing to do. So, I submitted the appropriate paperwork with Gallup and registered for the certification class—all so I could respond to my friend's text with: "I'll be certified on March 3rd!"

> **I couldn't afford to lose out on a technicality.**

Once the date for certification was "out there"—my departure from corporate had been determined and solidified. The few days of earned paid time off I had remaining were already dedicated to meetings or events for potential future clients, including the company in Virginia who had hired me, and the media company's "trial" retreat. For me to take a week to get CliftonStrengths® certified on March 3, I would need to have my position with the corporate job wrapped up at the end of February. And for me to feel secure about it all, I needed confirmation of the bonus and the money in my bank account by specific, fixed dates. Whereas, I really wanted to take the money and run, it was best to take a small pause before resigning. Mainly, I wanted to give my team and my boss as much notice as possible so they would have ample time for a smooth transition. I had no interest in burning bridges or leaving them in a lurch. It was a delicate timeline dance with most of the variables beyond my control.

Additionally, I had exactly zero clients officially lined up and contracted for CareerFrame. Zero. Hopefully, the corporate bonus would tide me over until I got things moving, if it came through. Sure, I had two possibilities in the hopper but neither quite translated to a monthly retainer. When I was honest with myself, resigning from corporate meant resigning from a steady paycheck, and the financial reality forced me to ask myself a question I often ask my clients: "How serious are you about taking this leap?" My answer: "I am taking this leap. No. Matter. What."

Resigned Calmness

When you step into your truth, the universe rewards you. I'd experienced divine timing a few times already but it seemed the universe was not done with me.

On January 17, my boss called to tell me I was getting my bonus: goal #1 achieved, right on time. The bonus hit my bank account on January 31: goal #2 achieved, also right on time. My plan was to resign the following week, on February 7. The day before, my boss called again; a rarity. Outside of our weekly 1x1s, we communicated primarily by text and email. She called to update me on a few things, one of which was that she was posting for another Director position and didn't want me to think anything about it: she was simply expanding the team.

This was it: my chance to say what I'd wanted to say all these many months. I said, "Actually, while I have you, do you have a minute? I have an update for you." Always friendly and one to lend an ear, she said, "Absolutely! What's up?" Very calmly, I told her "I have decided to leave." Very calmly right back, she said, "Ok. Talk to me."

I'm grateful that my boss and I had a great relationship from day one. We were always, and still are, no bullshit with each other and supportive of each other's dreams. I proceeded to tell her what she already knew: that my passion to get back to coaching had intensified over the last year. Whereas, I think she was happy to have me on her team and by her side, she knew my heart was elsewhere, and to her credit, she celebrated that and was fully supportive of my plan.

As anticipated, she asked how much time I could give her, and I relayed my need to be in class in March for the CliftonStrengths® certification. We were looking at three weeks, and of course, I was always available to her or the team if anyone needed anything beyond that. Even though I was ready to move on, I had every intention of being supportive because I cared about them. My team was an incredible group of people and, emotionally, it was hard to leave them. I loved them all but it was time for me to go.

Interestingly, when I finally officially resigned, I felt no panic, worry, fear, excitement, enthusiasm, nor happiness. There was simply calm. During the conversation with my boss, my soul was completely at peace, which only affirmed what I already knew: I was doing the right thing.

My soul was completely at peace, which only affirmed what I already knew: I was doing the right thing.

I had attended the media company's meeting in late January. The day after I resigned, on February 7, 2020, I received a signed contract from them for a yearlong partnership. When the universe asked how serious I was, and I resigned with zero income lined up, I showed it how serious I was indeed, and it rewarded me. Halle-freaking-lujah!

My last day in corporate was February 28. Two days later, I flew to Atlanta, Georgia to get my CliftonStrengths® certification. I was officially on my way back to CareerFrame, just in time for COVID-19 to shut the world down.

Damn Pandemic

Shortly after my return home from Atlanta, our country went into lockdown. Amongst the many things that were going through my brain and rocking all of our worlds, the schools shut down and went virtual. Like many, I felt so many emotions: sadness, confusion, fear, worry about my family, friends, and humanity in general. To be totally honest, one of the biggest emotions I felt was anger. My anger was totally, unapologetically selfish. It wasn't fair that just when I was full of excitement to have all day, Monday—Friday, to focus, plan, strategize, and prospect to re-launch CareerFrame into a legit business, instead, I had to become a full-time schoolteacher.

> **My anger was totally, unapologetically selfish.**

The whole thing was a total fucking unfair shit show, and moms across the world had a front row seat. We working moms found ourselves struggling to juggle educating our kids while maintaining an income, in addition to the default emotions of worrying about everyone's health and safety, and our sanity. Amidst the craziness, uncertainty, and turmoil of everything shutting down and going remote, leaving my steady paycheck seemed kind of, well, crazy. It was a huge test focused back to the question: how serious was I? At that moment in time, of course doubt crept into my psyche, and I questioned if I had made the right decision to leave the security of corporate. But I had made my choice, no matter what, and I was committed. Many moms were forced to leave their jobs entirely to focus on their kids. The push and pull was almost unbearable at times, and it drove me, and most of my mom friends, to intense drinking.

And I was one of the lucky ones. I worked from home and had the flexibility of when I worked. I was building my business so I didn't have to report to "the man," go to a hospital and risk my own safety like my doctor friends, or work for an essential business where if I didn't show up, I'd get fired. I bow down to the moms who scrambled like mad to ensure their kids were set up with their Google Meets, while running to their own, and I want to hug all of the moms who lost their jobs because they chose their kids first. We moms are constantly put in a position where we have to choose our kids over ourselves, and 98 percent of the time, we choose our kids. It's why many of us are depleted of our badass mama juiciness at the end of the day.

Andres and I had our fair share of arguments over whose work was more important and who was in charge of helping two kids—each on different schedules and one who learns differently—get on various electronic devices for school every day. Let alone, making sure the house was stocked with food and other supplies, everyone was fed, and the mid-day dishes were done. I've never run the dishwasher as many times as I did during lockdown. A few times, in the very beginning, I woke up at 5 a.m. to wait for a grocery store to open so I could get one of the five packages of toilet paper, if there were any left at all. My husband did step up from time to time, but like most moms, I felt like I did most of the heavy lifting.

Nevertheless, my family of four made the best of the situation, as best we could, and settled into the quaran-rou-tine of spending way too much time at home. By April, Andres suggested we go somewhere for a change of scenery. We decided to head up to New Mexico for a week, where my dad had a beautiful second home we called the "mountain house."

We got situated—Andres and I with our makeshift offices, his downstairs and mine at the kitchen table, and the kids with their makeshift desks, also at the kitchen table. I was still the designated primary teacher moonlighting as a working adult, for the remainder of the school year whose end thankfully, was fast approaching, but not fast enough.

Even though I was in the beautiful mountains, I was still pissed about the focused time I was losing for CareerFrame. I decided to simply let myself be angry and grieve the loss. I was beyond grateful for my partnership with the media company and yet, the contract was approximately one third of my corporate paycheck, so I had some prospecting work to do. Didn't it figure that when I decided to hold my nose and jump, a fucking pandemic shuts the world down and the wind gets knocked out of my pumped-up, motivated sail?

Tears for Fears

I had waited until my journey with Molly was complete at the end of 2019 before cashing in on the Results Coaching sessions I had as part of Tony's Mastery program. My new coach Jenn and I kicked things off in mid-January and I instantly appreciated her style. Being a part of the Tony world meant we both spoke the same no bullshit, "what action are you going to take?" language, and she had zero issues giving me healthy doses of this mentality. While in New Mexico, I scheduled a call with her.

When I heard her voice on the line, I fell apart on the call because the uncertainty with the state of the world and my born-again business was suddenly overwhelming. My self-talk was out of control, and my focus was in the shitter. Even after a year of intense, emotional work, my mind wanted to revert back to the familiar patterns of my "away" values. Jenn reminded me to, "Change your state of mind, shake it off, and breathe." She helped me snap back quickly, sending a flood of all that I had learned into my heart, and drowning out the lizard brain, but I was scared.

> Change your state of mind, shake it off, and breathe.

After our call, I grabbed my air pods, put them in my ears, and put on my Firewalker t-shirt from UPW. I walked out to the back deck, 30 feet above ground, stared off at the mountains, and noticed fear was circling like a vulture. I pressed play on my iTunes. With my arms up in a V-shape, I started bouncing up and down to "Let's Go" by Calvin Harris and Ne-Yo. Tears started streaming down my face as I listened to the words, hearing Ne-Yo sing to me that I should make no excuses, my time was running out, and it was not about what I had done; it was about what I was doing. It was now or never and LET'S GO!

I kept bouncing and crying, arms in a V, until fear got bored and flew away. When I felt it physically leave, I stopped the music, put my arms down, wiped the tears away, and stared out at the mountains. It was now or never and I simply had to trust the path of uncertainty. I saw no other way.

Our week in New Mexico turned into three. Dallas was still shut down for quarantine and the view was much better where we were, so we stayed and our family grew closer. Lucas and Lala settled into their routine and the four of us took long walks down to the creek at the bottom of the mountain. Lala fed the deer out back, and Lucas looked forward to playing with the thousands of moths outside the windows at nighttime. Andres took Lucas to the feed store for more deer food, and came home with two fish to add to our family. Lala named hers Silver and Lucas named his, well, Moth.

Most mornings, I woke up to watch the sunrise and the amazing hummingbirds dash around the forest. Andres and I had an Old Fashioned on the back deck almost every night. The mountain house became 10 times more special to us as we found new appreciations in a magical place that we had taken for granted in the past. It was our Covid sanctuary and we felt blessed.

I was determined to find beauty in the darkness and resolved to see things through a different lens. I was going to "plant in the winter to harvest in the spring." We were all going through a metaphorical winter with no end in sight. After all I had worked through—pain, fear, and the courage to take massive leaps—I was going to keep my heart focused on the fact that spring always follows winter. I decided I was not going to let the pandemic slow me down. I simply had to put on my big girl panties and trust this path. I had said that when my corporate lifeboat brought me to the shores of CareerFrame Island, I would burn the fucking boat. And that's what I had done. There was no going back. Only forward.

Find Your Juicy Life

Commit to taking the steps that will give you a leg up.
Investing in yourself is key and when you have goals of learning something, reading loads of books is a great start. Taking the extra step to take a course or get a certification could mean the difference between serious success or not. The thing about committing is, it's black or white. Once you commit to something, that's it. You're done and you go all in. Or you don't. My decision to get CliftonStrengths® certified was a further commitment to my CareerFrame path: a technical cherry on top of the emotional and mental work sundae I'd invested in through Molly's coaching and Tony's seminars. It gave me a strategic advantage in the marketplace as I began negotiating contracts and wooing clients.

Roll with the punches.
There is likely not a single person on earth who didn't have to step into the vast sea of uncertainty and fear that the Covid pandemic delivered. We were all tested and challenged in ways far outside of our comfort zones. And that is what life does. The only thing that is certain is uncertainty. When you find a way to simply trust the unknown path ahead of you, and focus only on what you can control, your life will simply unfold the way it's meant to. When your world is turned upside down, the only thing you can do is roll with it until it is made right again. Spring always follows the winter.

CHAPTER 10

TAKING CARE OF BUSINESS

> "Integrity is choosing courage over comfort."
> – *Brené Brown*

Tweaking

For my business to truly move forward and be successful, I had to get over my dislike of sales. After years of being in sales and account management for the travel industry, the dislike hadn't dissipated. In fact, it intensified through the work I did with my friend, the Sales Badass. During the short time I worked for her, one of our core methods was to get as many connections via LinkedIn as possible, and then paste a script into a message to request a phone call. The script felt super salesy, and it just wasn't my style. Whereas she was a machine at prospecting and booking calls, I was not.

Throughout my professional career, I preferred to focus on being a great sales *leader*, which allowed me to motivate the people selling versus doing the selling myself. Now, I was in a position where if I didn't sell for my business, no one was selling for it. LinkedIn was definitely the place where I wanted to make connections that could turn into business, but reaching out to total strangers, doing an elevator pitch, and asking for time on their calendar all at the same time didn't feel right to me. I had PTSD from cold-calling LinkedIn prospects, so how was I going to build my business with this mental block around selling?

I started noticing ads and posts in my LinkedIn feed about a program called Linkedprenueurs with Mark Firth[2]. Maybe this guy, if he was legit, could help me get past my mental block. I attended a free webinar with Mark and his friend Simon Lovell. They both talked about the Linkedpreneurs program with a small plug for Simon's program, Super High-Performance Formula. After watching these two guys show their authentic, non-douchey selves, I booked a one-on-one call with each of them. One offered a program that focused on building a muscle and skill for my business, and the other would help me continue along my transformation journey.

A week later, I enrolled in both of their programs. Something told me to leap but it didn't come without a pause. I still had a ways to go with my money mindset; I wasn't making the money I needed, and oh yeah, that mountain of debt was still towering. I knew from Molly and Tony that investing in myself would deliver the greatest ROI. I'd done the massive work with them and now it was time to do some tweaking.

Mark's class was centered on how to use emotional intelligence (EQ) when selling. In my opinion, it was such an obvious, genius approach. This type of selling doesn't feel like selling. It felt authentic and it worked. It also helped me get past my mental block of connecting to strangers via LinkedIn by posting something meaningful on their profile that was relevant to them and enhanced my chances of actually connecting with them via a phone call. Within the first two weeks of participating in Mark's course, I got three new clients using his method! The EQ approach to sales was what had been missing all along.

A fellow classmate in the program challenged me to post a series of videos on LinkedIn to educate viewers about my offerings. Posting videos of myself was way out of my comfort zone but I saw the value in her suggestion. Scared as hell, I recorded a short video on my iPhone to announce: "Starting next week, and running every Tuesday and Thursday, I will be kicking off *Framing Your Strengths*, a series of snippets and tidbits about each talent theme in CliftonStrengths®."

Framing Your Strengths launched in July and ran for 17 weeks. I landed

[2] https://markfirthonline.com/

a few clients because of the series and had a lot of fun reading the many comments from engaged viewers. All of the fears and shitty self-talk that had blocked my progress in the past were silenced, and I was on my way. I had learned a new technique, put it into motion, and started to see the results I wanted.

The Sword of Pride

Simon's Super High Performance Formula[3] program kicked off in tandem with Mark's Linkedpreneurs program. I was one of six participants and the only female in the group. I will say I loved how those dudes were stepping up to seek tough love and ass-kicking coaching from Simon because his program is no joke, starting with his accountability protocol.

Every morning during the six-week program, we each had to log in to the system, before noon, and fill out an accountability form. If you neglected to fill out the form one day, or even if you filled it out *after* noon, you were kicked out of the system. To get back in, you had to do something big and bold. Simon would give the culprit three choices of activities he deemed appropriate. But if you got kicked out of the system three times, you were kicked out of the program for good with no refund. Obviously, no one wanted that!

One day, I missed the noon deadline, got kicked out of the system, and had to pick my redemptive action to get back in. Of the three actions Simon gave me, I chose to go live on Facebook and tell the community why I was not accountable. I leaned in and owned my mistake because I had no desire to forfeit the four figures I'd already invested. After my first offense, I was vigilant for the remainder of the program.

In the first week, Simon introduced us to David Hawkins' book, *Letting Go*. I listened to it on Audible during workouts and long walks around the neighborhood. Hawkins talks about how to surrender emotions that are not serving you and keeping you in a low energetic vibration. To visualize this concept, he introduces his Map of Consciousness in which shame sits at the bottom of the chart with the lowest energetic vibration and enlightenment is at the top with the highest energetic vibration. Hawkins

[3] https://www.simonlovell.com/

walks the reader through the process of letting go of low vibrational emotions—apathy, depression, grief, fear, desire, anger and pride—in order to step into the higher vibrational emotions—courage, acceptance, love and peace.

The book put a big mirror up in front of me. Staring back was anger and, especially, pride. Whereas I knew where the anger had come from after years of trauma around loss, I wasn't quite sure where this pride problem was coming from. And it wasn't the type of "I'm really proud of myself" pride. This was the ugly "look how great I am" pride. I thought it through and realized that pride showed up whenever I was over-compensating for my insecurities, and apparently, I had a mountain of them. Pride was the puppeteer to my ego. It's what wedged its way into, and almost destroyed, my friendship with the Sales Badass.

Pride was the puppeteer to my ego.

In the second week of the program, we were presented with an exercise to test our courage, which falls in the middle of Hawkins' Map of Consciousness. Simon insisted we could not move forward until we posted a confessional video on Facebook to our entire community. This video was to be about something no one knew about us. We had to let it all out, or let it go, if you will. I needed an extra day to process this exercise because even though I consider myself to be a highly courageous person, I had to find the courage to initiate the exercise on courage itself.

I thought through what I wanted to tell hundreds of people on Facebook, and decided, I had to do this. Yet, there was something else I simply had to do first. I had to reconnect with the Sales Badass. She had given me a job, paid me well, and become my dear friend. We were glued at the hip for a solid year, and now, I was ready to own that I had been the asshole who pushed her away with pride as my backer. I sent her a text to see if she would make some time to connect with me on FaceTime. It was important that we saw each other's faces when I said what I intended to say. She was likely thinking, "WTF?" since my text was totally out of the blue. But being her usual, gracious self, she agreed to talk the next morning.

Before the call, I went for a jog, took a shower, and sat down to record my video for Facebook. In a ten-minute segment, I informed the audience what this was about and for, and warned them that I wanted to make a few confessions. I quickly recapped my path up until that point; how I had felt unfulfilled and wanted to focus on coaching, so I hired a coach of my own. I explained how she helped me become a better version of myself and get back to what my heart desired. I talked about the hard and painful path to a rewarding transformation, and how I was adopting the new psychology of a business owner.

After introducing Simon's immersive program, I admitted to the camera that I felt something had been blocking me from fully stepping into my power with my business. I shared how hard it was to do the video, and then admitted that I had had an immense fear of loss. That same fear had fueled an overpowering need to control everything in my life. I talked about losing my mom when I was 9, remembering the moment they closed her casket, and knowing that I would never see her again. My first heart wall went up (and was guarded in its vault by my magician). Then, only five years later, my high school boyfriend died and another heart wall went up (another vault). Many of my Facebook friends were old high school friends and acquaintances who would remember that traumatic time we all endured.

I shared that my stepmom, whom I adored, died when I was 23, and three years later, my stepsister also died, adding more heart walls and vaults in an already crowded broken heart. I talked about how my heart was protected out of fear of more loss. That fear, anger and pride had gotten in the way of a lot of things.

I confessed to being a know-it-all, insecure hypocrite who tells others not to judge; yet I judged all the time. How ironic was it that I feared loss and tried to control future loss by sabotaging relationships. If people got too close, I would subconsciously induce loss because it was familiar and what I thought I deserved. Through the work I'd done with Molly and at Tony's seminars, I realized that I needed to forgive myself, and interestingly, I told myself to forgive people for treating me poorly as a response to how I had treated *them*. My behavior stemmed from the fear of loss and also rejection. Rejection triggered me into thinking, "Of course, you're rejecting me. I'm losing you. All I ever get is loss." It was complicated.

Simon's program was about emotional and energetic intelligence. When we hold on to trauma, it becomes a black, muddy, sluggish ball of shit that blocks us from raising our energetic vibration. We have to get it out of our bodies because if we don't, it keeps us small. Most of the people who would watch this video would likely never say that I have a small personality or am small in anyway; so I told them that my big personality was sometimes an act to cover up for feeling small, and not wanting others to see it. I told them that my husband was a gift to me as I had sabotaged amazing, healthy intimate relationships in the past because I didn't think I deserved them. With Andres, he never budged in the face of my sometimes "insecure psycho girl" behavior. He was my rock, my teacher, and a huge blessing who saw me for my bigness, not smallness.

Finally, I apologized to anyone I had hurt, upset, pushed away or insulted.

I concluded by asking the viewers to hold me accountable for letting go of my fear of loss, fear of rejection and especially pride. If they heard or saw me being prideful, they were to call me out on it, and help me make the shift. I wrapped it up by saying this video was not about beating up on myself; it was a way for me to let go of the emotions that were holding me back. It was a vehicle to shift my energy and release my fears.

The response to the video was incredible. It got more views than I imagined, and people reached out via text, IM, or through the comments. Many of the messages were filled with love and supportive encouragement. Some said they were inspired by my bravery and encouraged to take some kind of action themselves. One of the messages was from an ex-boyfriend from high school who had been verbally abusive toward me throughout our relationship. He left a confessional comment of his own in my feed for everyone to see. In it, he acknowledged how hurtful he'd been to me back then and apologized. He thanked me for who I was to him and said I'd helped to make him the happily married husband and father (of four) that he is today. His words were heartfelt and deeply touching. I guess when you do something courageous, it's contagious.

When you do something courageous, it's contagious.

Before posting the video on Facebook, I called the Sales Badass on FaceTime at our agreed upon time. It was important to me that I make things right with her before releasing a mass apology to anyone I had offended in the past. When she picked up, I smiled at her, thanked her for agreeing to talk with me, and went straight into the reason for my call. I owned how I treated her, how I had talked about her behind her back, how I had judged the choices she made, and asked her for forgiveness. She graciously accepted my request, which was no surprise because that's just the type of person she is.

As we talked, I began to feel lighter. We quickly picked up where we had left off and got caught up on the details of our lives. I admitted to my original and ludicrous rejection of our rental house because her old house was next door. She said, "But I didn't even live there anymore," to which I replied, "I KNOW! What the actual fuck with my thought track?" We both got a good laugh at my immature reaction and continued to reconnect deeper and at a fast pace as if there was so much time to make up for. She's an incredibly loving person and it felt amazing to open up and be completely honest about why our friendship faded. Our conversation put me at ease, and I knew that apologizing to her and recording the courage video for Facebook would set me free from that black ball of muddy crap I'd been carrying.

Taking these two actions had a ripple effect. Not only had I let go of my ugly pride, I got my dear friend back. She asked what I was up to professionally, and I told her that, though things were slow due to the pandemic, I was beyond happy to be back in the driver's seat full-time for CareerFrame. Ever generous and helpful, she proceeded to introduce me to people she had partnered with and overall trusted professionally.

One of those introductions was to Lou Diamond, the founder of ThriveLoud, who invited me to be a guest on his podcast, an opportunity I leapt at. It happened fast and furiously and the next thing I knew, Lou was interviewing me about my business and, more specifically, what I did and why. He gave me a platform to share how I wanted to inspire people to reframe their thinking and become better versions of themselves. Being the pro that he is, he made me feel totally relaxed and confident, and we had a blast doing the interview.

Two months later, Lou sent a sneak peek of the podcast recording before it went live. I listened to it when I was out for a walk and found myself smiling from ear to ear, proud of how I sounded, and even prouder of what I had shared. That was the kind of pride I wanted to feel!

At the end of the interview, Lou faded to my go-to inspirational song, "Let's Go" by Calvin Harris and Ne-Yo, which gave me chills from head to toe. Something in that moment told me everything was going to be all right. Hell, it was going to be better than all right.

Obi-Wan

My work with Linkedpreneurs had produced beautiful fruit and I was starting to get juiced up through new clients. My two big client retainer engagements were going well and I had two new Dallas clients about to ignite. I was focused on building the business but had to face the fact that I was not what anyone would call an experienced, strategic entrepreneur. Meaning, I had no business skills or experience when it came to owning and operating a successful profitable business. Up until then, I had simply been making shit up as I went along, hoping CareerFrame didn't look like a total joke.

> **I was not what anyone would call an experienced, strategic entrepreneur.**

To up the ante, I started to invest in basic foundational systems for the business such as a proper automated invoicing system versus crafting fancy excel spreadsheets and PDFing them to clients (good God). I bought subscriptions to Zoom, SurveyMonkey, LinkedIn Premiere, DocuSign (for all of those contracts), Stripe, upgraded Adobe, G Suite, and bought a new laptop. Along the way, my phenomenal bookkeeper was instrumental in guiding me to the next level.

Despite all of the investments and upgrades, something was still missing, and I realized it was a strategic advisor. I needed someone to mentor me towards killer success. However, the trouble was, I had no idea who it would be. I put it out to the universe and decided I was going to manifest that shit; the perfect person would appear in due time.

My intuition told me to reconnect with Lou. With no agenda or timeframe, I reached out anyway and we hopped on a Zoom. After the initial friendly chit chat, I said, "You might be wondering why I reached out and, to tell you the truth, I have no idea! My gut told me to contact you and so I did." He laughed and we simply let the conversation take us wherever it was intended.

Organically, and in the context of our discussion, I mentioned I was looking for a mentor. He was intrigued to hear more, so I told him what I needed and then said, "Wait, are *you* the mentor I've been looking for?" He laughed and said he had no idea but he'd ponder it. The very next day, he sent an email saying he would love to mentor me; we should outline the specifics and determine guidelines.

A few weeks later, Lou and I officially kicked off a partnership with scheduled weekly calls during which he guided me through how to create a profitable, legitimate, professional consulting business. As a result of our calls, he boosted my confidence, helped me craft stellar proposals, adjust my pricing, own my worth and the value I brought to clients, and overall helped me step into my power as a solo-preneur. Lou set me up to make more money than I had ever imagined possible. Obi-wan was officially training the young Jedi to become a master.

Find Your Juicy Life

Own your shit.
A primary way to juice up your life is to own when you are the asshole getting in your own way through limiting beliefs. Find a way to be authentically you, even when that means you need to admit to someone, or many people, that you have been off-putting and haven't let yourself be vulnerable. When you are vulnerable, you open up the opportunity to bring trust into your life. Call yourself out in areas that drag you and others down, address it, learn from it, heal it, and go forth being awesomely you.

Identify skills you want to learn and invest in teachers.
We all have areas where we need to grow and not all of them are emotional, mental, spiritual, or physical. Perhaps you need to learn a trade or hone a skill? What do you want to be better at either in your career or with a hobby? Find what excites you and then find classes, teachers, and gurus to show you how to build on your existing skills and level up.

Get a mentor.
A mentor is different from a coach. Whereas a coach will kick your ass into taking action, a mentor is a trusted advisor that has gone before you on the exact path you want to walk down yourself. They guide you by modeling behavior. They will show you how they got where they are, and if it's a place you want to be, they will help you get there the way they got there. Finding someone you trust, who has patience and who will be your biggest cheerleader is a key component of professional success.

CHAPTER 11

MASTERING

> "What you get by achieving your goals is not as important as what you become by achieving your goals."
> – Zig Ziglar

Solo Plunge

The first year of going all in with my consulting business was bright and inspiring, despite what was going on in the world. Jessica and I had planned to reunite in San Diego that summer for the final two seminars in our Mastery journey—Life and Wealth Mastery—but Covid had other plans, and everyone stayed home.

Engaging with my Results coach and having Lou as my mentor gave me just enough juice to sustain the momentum of my solo-preneur trajectory. I finally started to feel like I was stepping into my professional destiny. My engagement with the media company was successful, and they wanted to renew for 2021. Another client was extending their agreement, and I had several executive coaching opportunities lined up. At DWD in Florida, Tony had asked us to write down our income goals for one, three and five years. In 10 short months, I had hit my one-year goal by continuing to invest in myself and stretch in new directions.

> **I finally started to feel like I was stepping into my professional destiny.**

I'd come a long way in a short time but I still wanted more. It was time to get back to the world of Mastery and put the final touches on my journey. During the height of the pandemic, Tony had been busy building a massive virtual studio in Palm Beach. His ingenuity and creativity was in the spirit of maintaining a beautiful and juiced-up state of mind. For the first time ever, his thousands of raving fans could experience the energetic and inspiring vibe of his seminars from the comfort of their homes. The inaugural virtual seminar would be *Life Mastery*, seven months after it was originally scheduled.

Jessica had other things going on in her life at the time, so I decided to continue on the Mastery path solo this time. With Lucas and Lala back to in-person school and Andres working on his own business, I headed once again to my dad's house in New Mexico, solo on this excursion, too. With a house in the mountains to myself for a few days, I planned on another total Tony immersion.

Life Mastery was a deep dive into wellness: physical health and fitness, cognitive, and emotional. With a refrigerator stocked with fruits and veggies in preparation for a four-day cleanse during the seminar, I mentally prepared myself for the big event that would kick things off the first night: the *Life Mastery* ice bath challenge.

Jesse Itzler, the husband of Spanx founder Sara Blakely, led us through the mental and physical mechanics of immersing ourselves in a freezing cold bathtub. The point of an ice bath is to forcefully constrict the blood vessels, flush out waste products, reduce inflammation and breakdown tissue. Subsequently, when the tissue warms up again, increased blood flow speeds circulation, and a healing process is accelerated. We were to sit in the bath for two minutes, cameras on, in front of 4,000 other people from around the world, so we could all experience it together LIVE. Fun, right?

As I dumped bags and bags of ice into a bathtub filled with cold water, I thought, "Am I completely out of my mind?" I gingerly stuck a toe in before getting in all the way. Wearing a swimsuit under a T-shirt, I stayed there for two full minutes and yelled in frozen agony, "I am OUTSTANDING! I am OUTSTANDING! It's so HOT in here! It's so hot—it's STEAMING! I am OUTSTANDING!" #poorattemptatamindhack #completelyoutofmymind

When the two minutes were up, every inch of my body felt like it was being pricked with pins and needles. I definitely felt the increased blood flow rushing back to my capillaries, and it was intense. I dried off, put on my coziest sweats, and within 30 minutes, my body felt the most amazing it had felt in I couldn't even remember when. I was pretty sure I would never do such a thing again, but I enjoyed the amazing feeling. Turns out, three nights later, I did the entire ice bath routine again, just to prove to myself that I could. Call me crazy.

The rest of the seminar was a throwback to the "regular" Tony events with long 13-hour days. Only this time, we were all jumping around on Zoom and participating in breakout rooms. We shared stories about our personal journey, health, and professional goals. Overall, the meetings made me appreciate my life.

Like past Tony events, day three brought about a breakthrough for me. As I cracked wide open, my tears this time were attached to pure joy. It almost hurt to cry from a place of joy versus a place of trauma and sadness, which had been my wellspring for decades. Standing in the living room of the mountain house, these new tears streamed down my face in celebration of how far I had come and all the work that went into it. I thought about how much I loved and appreciated my family, and how I wanted to use my story to inspire my clients and others who were willing to listen and learn.

It almost hurt to cry from a place of joy versus a place of trauma and sadness, which had been my wellspring for decades.

I felt like I was finally "mastering life." I had made decisions that served me, unapologetically. My friends, my family, and everyone around me gave me the space to do so, even if sometimes reluctantly. They acknowledged and tried to understand that the intentions behind my decisions were never in any attempt to hurt them if my decisions had in fact done so. They were all an attempt to find a better, happier version of myself so I could finally really show up in life, as the wife, mom, sister, daughter, niece, friend, and coach they all needed me to be.

Check, Please!

When I got back to Dallas, pumped up by another Tony event, I continued to build the foundation for my coaching business. When I checked my master invoice tracker, I smiled in disbelief. Companies were finding me, hiring me for leadership coaching and CliftonStrengths® workshops, and my little consulting engine was gaining momentum despite the pandemic.

During my journey with Molly, one of the things we worked on was visualizing my financial future as a coach and leadership consultant. I remember, I bought a giant novelty check on Amazon, made it out to myself, wrote a large six-figure number on the check, dated it "by December 31, 2021," and hung it on the wall in my home office. Hell, if it worked for Jim Carey, it could work for me. Apparently, he wrote himself a check for $10 million dollars (my check was for a little less) and carried it around in his wallet. Not too much later, Jim got the $10 million when he landed his role in *Dumb and Dumber*.

When I wrote the fantasy check to myself, the number in the dollar box seemed impossible, like a dream. I stared at it for most of 2019, all of 2020 and into 2021. But as Audrey Hepburn said, "Impossible says 'I'm possible.'" and when I looked at my invoice tracker and the contracted clients lined up for the year ahead, I had already surpassed that number on my novelty check. Just as I had surpassed my one-year financial goal in 10 months, I was now poised to surpass my three-year goal 13 months after leaving corporate, with signed contracts in the hopper, and no intention of slowing down!

I continued to focus on momming hard with Lucas and Lala and surviving Covid life with the family. I had found a way to take care of them *and* support my clients, whom I adored, by rocking the virtual office trend. Having been a remote corporate leader for 14 years didn't hurt the cause.

Even though I was ahead of schedule with my financial goals and had worked through so many limiting beliefs, my money mindset still needed some tweaking. It was not even remotely lost on me that Andres and I still carried debt. And yet, we continued to spend money on travel and invest in my business and self-growth, choices I will never regret. Most smart people with any financial sense would probably not agree with how we managed our money but we weren't making reckless, dumb decisions at every turn. We simply made decisions as needed to support our businesses, our family, our interests, and ourselves. We had debt and we wanted to LIVE. Thanks to the success both Andres and I were seeing, the debt tally was slowly going down. We still wanted to have fun and live life, so we kept an eye on the finances and got better at establishing some sort of balance.

Money Flows

The key to amassing wealth is asking, "How can I add more value?" Tony's forthcoming *Wealth Mastery*, the final leg of my Mastery journey, would no doubt give me some valuable insight on the topic. A few months after *Life Mastery*, I logged back into the virtual Tony world for the end of my Mastery journey. Talking about wealth, the topic where I needed ongoing mindset shifts and growth was the perfect ending. Tony's Zoom crew wasted no time diving right into the topic by telling us first and foremost, "If you can't live with uncertainty, you won't master wealth." Well, hell.

Uncertainty had not been my friend over the years but I was determined to master wealth, even though I had a residual "lack mindset" when it came to money. I had been telling myself for decades that wealth was all about dollars and cash when in fact, it was about value: mentally, emotionally, physically, spiritually, and *then* financially. I had to accept the concept that no amount of money would actually make me wealthy.

Once again, Tony touched on cognitive, physical, and emotional mastery, as he had at past events. The repetition of new belief systems across his seminars was by design. In my breakout Zoom room, we explored our old financial stories by writing down our money mindsets up until that point. Then, we were asked to write a new financial story, reframing the old mindset with intention and visualizing where we would be in the future.

In the middle of the exercise, I ran up to my office, grabbed a black sharpie, and wrote a new target date on my gigantic novelty check: July 31, 2021. I only had three months to the day to achieve my next BHAG (big hairy audacious goal). I also wrote in big letters under my goal amount, "after taxes," essentially upping the new target amount by six figures. Intention and visualization: check!

Racing back downstairs to rejoin the session, we talked about IRAs, compound investing, Bitcoin, and how to be deliberative with money—a concept very foreign to my activator brain. With debt still lingering, and exhausted from years of carrying it, I made some bold goals to get that shit paid off. I also made bold goals to invest in marketing for my business and support my path to financial freedom along with being wealthy in every aspect.

Most importantly, I was done with the shame of it all. I spent years shaming myself, and occasionally Andres, for "letting ourselves" go into debt. *Wealth Mastery* was geared towards freedom in every way, especially financial. Critically for me, the seminar was successful because it gave me the knowledge and power to switch my mindset away from the emotional baggage the debt represented and toward value and quality of life. All of those years, Andres and I wanted value and quality of life. If having debt meant we would experience life, then we had succeeded, and shame had no place in our lives anymore.

Shame had no place in our lives anymore.

Wealth Mastery was the cherry on top of the proverbial Tony Robbins Mastery transformation sundae. I had come immensely far with my money scarcity mindset from *Unleash the Power Within* and that day I handed my credit card over to Veronica to purchase the Mastery journey.

When she said, "No shit, Carrie. This will change your life. I tripled my business as a result of the program. You cannot and will not see it now, but please know, all of the success and happiness you want is coming your way through this journey."

"Well, no shit, Veronica! It did change my life!" How right she was.

Shortly after *Wealth Mastery*, I signed a new travel client for the rest of the year. I was stoked to have a toe back in the industry I knew so well, while also being in charge of my own business. With the travel company on board and the various other workshops and contracts I had lined up for the rest of the year, I went back to that giant novelty check on my office wall. With my black sharpie, I put an equally giant check mark next to the BHAG dollar amount I aimed for by July 31. It was July 8. Originally, I gave myself five years to accomplish that goal but I got there in only 16 months.

Just as Veronica promised, I had tripled my corporate salary as a result of my transformation journey. I stared at the check on the wall in disbelief, beaming with pride, the good kind of pride this time!

The Soul Path

When I met with the Intuitive—before working with Molly or diving into Tony's world—she told me that whenever I operated within honor, integrity, and courage, I would be on my soul path. Alternatively, whenever I operated without honor, integrity, and courage, I would find myself astray and need to redo whatever I had done under different emotions and intentions.

As I started to step into my professional and personal potential, my business grew, and with it, my confidence. The idea that I was on my soul path began to feel true. This path gave me the juice I had craved to make each day count, to be present with Andres, Lucas and Lala, to be all in with whatever I was doing and whoever I was with.

In thinking about the values that allowed me to walk my soul path, it occurred to me that honor is about the past. During the journey towards my juicy life, I realized how brutal my inner critic had been to my past selves. Self-talk thrives on rehashing bad decisions, mistakes made and missteps. The past is a super convenient fuel source for the inner critic. It provides ammunition all day, backed with historic evidence. Self-talk doesn't like when we focus on present circumstances in the moment. Beating ourselves up over things we did in the past keeps us small and stuck, but when we honor our past selves, something changes.

A perfect example of how this works showed up for me during a meditation exercise one day. For literally three decades, I beat myself up over, of all the crazy things, my damn SAT score. (I literally do not know a single person who got a lower SAT score than I did.) Admitting as much in writing, all these years later, doesn't erase the feelings I carried around for years about it. Even though, I like to point out, high-test scores and college degrees do not necessarily equate to smarts or success. I'm proof after all, and I'm in good company with Steve Jobs and Bill Gates. Clearly, we're all in the same league. Sarcasm aside, I was tired of holding on to this lack of kindness towards myself. After all, the SAT is a high school test. My career and I were far past that.

When we honor our past selves, something changes.

During the meditation and visualization exercise, my current self went back to mentally hug the 17-year-old me and tell her it was all going to be more than okay. I admitted I'd been too hard on her and didn't factor in all that she was up against back then. Younger Carrie was still mourning the death of her 9th grade boyfriend, Kevin, who was hit by a car riding his bike home from the gym. As a result of this trauma, and the loss of her mother only five years earlier, younger Carrie pushed everyone she loved away. She started hanging out with a different crowd, one that was not as upstanding as her friends to-date. She subconsciously assumed that if they didn't mean as much to her, it wouldn't hurt as bad if they died or left. Younger Carrie was robotic for the rest of high school. She wouldn't let anyone too close. She dated loser after loser. When the occasional great guy came along, she sabotaged the relationship so she wouldn't get hurt in the end.

The last thing Younger Carrie cared about was the SAT. She didn't prepare or study for it, and she despised standardized tests. Consequentially, she bombed and was only accepted to one school, Stephen F. Austin University in Nacogdoches, Texas, and just barely. She didn't care; she was just checking boxes.

My current self sought forgiveness, and through this powerful meditative exercise, Younger Carrie granted it. I was able to let go of decades of self-loathing and step into honoring that girl who contributed to making me who I am today. It may sound funny that I had such a profound experience around a freaking SAT score but trauma is trauma. When you do the mental work to heal it, there is a release, and suddenly, there is space to recognize the badass you have become.

Trauma is trauma. When you do the mental work to heal it, there is a release.

Integrity is about the present. When we live in the moment, we can see the truth. The tricky part is, we must heal the past and allow ourselves to step into and embrace who we are today. Once I honored my younger self and the whole SAT fiasco/crap story I had been telling myself, I could see who I was and express gratitude to my present self. The truth is that my college path didn't matter. What I do and who I am has zero to do with the degree I got from UT Austin, where I ultimately wound up, and my SAT score didn't mean jack shit. It was not a reflection of my potential, and it doesn't define me.

My truth today—in the present—is that I love what I do. I love working with my clients, and I love that I'm still growing along the way. It's why I always show up to every engagement full of energy and integrity, and it's why I can look myself in the mirror and know who I really am. I have learned to trust that my mistakes were, and will continue to be, part of the path.

As they say, the truth will set you free. Reframing your reality from a negative into a positive propels you forward towards the beauty of now. In the present, there is calm. The past can lead us to depression, if we let it. The present allows us to decide who we are, why it matters, and it launches us forward, full of integrity.

Courage is about the future. It's about being scared to do something and doing it anyway. It shows up to translate what fear is really trying to tell us. Unless we are in literal danger for our lives, fear is simply tapping us on the shoulder to show us the path we are supposed to be on. We turn fear into something ugly because it dares to reveal what we are actively avoiding.

Remember how loud fear was howling at me right after I resigned from corporate and the pandemic hit? Thankfully, Courage showed up too and whispered that fear was not there to scare me; it was there to get my attention and motivate me to keep going in the direction I was being pulled.

Honor, integrity and courage as guiding values on the soul path make complete sense to me. So much so, they became the foundation of my ReFrame Mastery coaching program and my online ecourse, ReFrame Mastery *Kickstarter*. In this framework, I outline a seven-step process to help people get on the path to reframing for the ideal: to take negative thoughts and turn them into positive action by going through the past, present, and future. The program is a great point of entry for people who 1) have never worked with a coach before, and/or 2) feel stuck, can't explain why, but want more out of their lives. It kickstarts participants to the next level of longer-term work with a coach and/or mentor. Through my own journey, I've learned that when we honor the past, have integrity in the present, and courage for the future, we will learn how to go ALL IN to juice up our lives.

Find Your Juicy Life

Visualize your goals.
There's something incredibly powerful and motivating about having your goals written out and tacked on the wall. It's a daily reminder of what you're reaching for. Just looking at them, and thinking about them, makes it more likely they will come to fruition, and you might be surprised at how quickly. Grab a sharpie and write your goals, large and in charge, and hang them somewhere that you will see every day. If you believe them, you will achieve them.

Assess your money mindset.
Do you believe you are worthy of achieving your goals and living into your potential, or are you overly comfortable sitting in a place of lack? What you believe has a funny way of morphing into what you are. Check yourself and adjust as necessary. Again, if you want more, write down what you want and put it on your wall or your bathroom mirror so you see it all the time. Remember the Henry Ford quote: "Whether you think you can or can't, you're right!" Only you will stand in your way of reaching the goals you want, financially and otherwise.

Take an online course.
There are so many amazing courses and online programs you can jump into as a way of saying a huge YES to your growth. Resources like Teachable, edX.com and so many others are available to you. If you're interested in learning how to step into your own Soul Path, I invite you to check out my online course Reframe Mastery *Kickstarter*. Visit www.carriefabris.com to find the course and reframe any situation so you can fill up that juice tank.

CHAPTER 12

A JUICY LIFE

> "He who has a why to live for can bear almost any how."
> -*Friedrich Nietzsche*

After all the ups, downs, and sloppy sideways I endured for five years, I officially experienced the feeling of fulfillment. I found joy like I'd never seen it before. All of my life, it was there, waiting for me to come claim it, and I finally did, both professionally and personally.

My life wouldn't be anywhere near as juicy as it is without my A.L.L.— Andres, Lucas and Lala. My husband has been my rock, and even though I paused for a moment in time to let ME be my why, at the core of my why are my beautiful, smart, sweet, funny, crazy, holy terrors, best huggers children.

I imagine all moms have a similar pile of adjectives to describe their kids but here's the thing with my two. One of them chose me, the other one saved me, and they are both my teachers. Without them, my juicy transformation might never have happened. My children, and my reframed interpretation of fulfillment, are what keep me going. They are why I must put my own oxygen mask on first, so I can be strong and present and available, so I can help them navigate their own paths in this world.

Captain Fantastic

Without knowing one single detail about Lucas or how he came into this world, the Intuitive I met with years ago told me, "Your son is profoundly gifted. He chose you. And he waited for you to slow down and be ready before he decided to come be your son on this earth." Amazed by her observation, I told her that it took 19 months to get pregnant with him. And, I didn't mean to be crass, but that was a google-tillion amount of sperm, and this child was the result.

Again, she said, "I know. He chose you. You were the mommy he wanted, and he was not going to present himself until you slowed down and were ready. He is an amazing teacher of patience for you." She had no idea how understated that comment was. When I saw the Disney movie, *Soul*, I immediately knew that Lucas was once a little soul, looking down on earth, searching for where he was supposed to belong, just as they were depicted in the movie. Unsolicited and in *his* own words, Lucas has told me more than once, "I went to the mommy store and chose you." Whoa.

Unsolicited and in *his* own words, Lucas has told me more than once, "I went to the mommy store and chose you."

Not a single day passes that I do not reflect on how connected I am with Lucas, and Lord knows, he has indeed taught me patience I never knew I had. Early on with him, I perfected what I call the "mom stare"—the kind of stare that says, in the most lovingly, gentle way, "Kid, do not fuck with me. I will win. You will lose. And you can sit there and wonder what the hell I'm thinking until you change your attitude!"

There have been many, many times when this mom stare has come out, like all the times Lucas was determined to be as stubborn as humanly possible, pretended to not comprehend what I asked of him, and gave me serious attitude. One time in particular, he was sitting at the bar in the kitchen, and we were working on flash cards with sight words. Now, I knew for a fact that my son knew how to spell and say the word "like" as displayed on a flash card I held up, just as he knew how to spell and say "make" and "good" and "play." So, why he full-on refused to demonstrate his academic excellence was not only beyond me, but also really pissed me off.

After about 15 minutes of fighting me over this one stupid word, I calmly gathered the deck of flashcards, gently shuffled them, put them all in one hand and dramatically slammed the deck down on the counter, which made him jump with his eyes wide open. I said absolutely nothing. I simply gave him the mom stare, poured myself a glass of wine, mom stared at him again with a little head tilt that said "you want a piece of me?" and walked away leaving him sitting there wondering what was going through my head. Moms, this is pretty much gold in the mommy vault. It's absolute torture for a little kid to not know what their mom is thinking, especially with *that* look on her face.

I went into the living room, sipped my wine, played a game on my phone and after 15 minutes, went back into the kitchen. When I rounded the corner, Lucas was still sitting right where I left him at the counter. He leaned to the side a little and carefully asked, "Mommy? Are you still mad?" With my best poker face, I replied, "Are you going to tell me your sight words?" "Yes! Yes, I will!" he said.

Maintaining the poker face but laughing hysterically in my head like Maleficent, I sauntered over, grabbed the deck of cards, and held them up one by one. He didn't miss a beat. Lucas said, "like," "make," "cake," "good," "play," "stop," and on and on as if he was the grand champion of the sight word competition. Uh huh. When he was done, I leaned in, smiled and said, "See, baby? Was that so hard? Great job, now go play!" The mom stare is money. It's a genius move if I do say so myself. I sipped my wine and cheered myself. #winning

Lucas was diagnosed with learning disabilities when he was 4 years old. Since then, he has been in and out of speech therapy, occupational therapy, cognitive behavioral therapy, feeding classes, social skills classes, reading programs, and of course, the Structure Program that we sold our house for him to attend. Every appointment, every coordinated effort to get him where he needed to be within my or Andres' work schedules, every dollar spent—a lot of dollars spent—have been worth it. Lucas thrives in his own way and whereas I might have sounded harsh with the flashcards, he's a smart kid when he puts effort into what he's doing. He learns on his own individual education plan. I love this for him and often think he is one of the lucky ones for getting the opportunity to learn at his pace, in whatever way is best for him. The highs have been really high while the lows have been really low, full of frustration, and occasionally, sadness.

The day a psychologist confirmed what I already knew about my son was one of the saddest days of my life. The moment of a diagnosis is scary as hell. I wondered: Will he go to college? Will he get married if he chooses to? Will he be able to live successfully on his own? Today, it's a resounding "yes" to all of those questions and possibilities; however, when we first learned about his learning differences, they weighed heavily on my mommy heart. I was sad for both of us, and yet, he has never given his challenges a second thought. It's simply who he is. He has taught me so much with that outlook; he has worked his ass off in therapies, tutoring (which he almost never complains about), and is a total rock star in every way. He is adored at his school; almost everyone knows who Lucas is and about his passions. The teachers and his schoolmates lean into who he is, handsome as ever, always silly, quirky and the sweetest boy. He's the big man on campus, and I can't wait to see what he becomes.

There are many days when I'm beyond grateful that my son is how he is. He is not in a wheelchair, non-verbal or struggling with a disease or diagnosis that will keep him from living on his own, caring for himself, or living a "typical" life as he grows older. I know many moms who have children with health situations that will keep them tethered to each other for the rest of the mom's life. I'm in pure awe of those moms and their strength, and it's always a reminder to appreciate what I have in my kiddo. Even when we go through hard times, and our hard times are valid and shouldn't be compared to others', there is always a situation that could be worse. There have been times with Lucas that have been challenging, just like his path to conception was, and it's been worth every minute.

Above all things on this planet, Lucas loves fans: ceiling fans, box fans, anything that remotely resembles a fan. He knows that National Ceiling Fan Day is on September 18 and yes, that is a real thing (who the hell knew?). Lucas first discovered a ceiling fan when he was 2-months-old. I caught him lying in his nap nanny staring up at it one day, mesmerized.

Later, his first words would be "dada," "mama" and "that's a fan!" When potty training time came around, any time Lucas had a successful poop in the potty, Andres and I would load him up in the car and head to Home Depot. We marched straight back to the fans section, I'd set a timer for 15 minutes, and we studied and discussed all the different types of fans. My boy was in heaven, and highly motivated to aim his poops appropriately.

For the next decade, as we lovingly supported Lucas' biggest passion, our family came to know everything there is to possibly know about fans. So much so, that one day in the school drop-off line, a crazy idea came my way. We had recently lost a school library book and the librarian was opening car doors that morning.

I hollered out the window, "Ugh, I'm so sorry! I have no idea what happened to that book. I'll send a check tomorrow!"

She hollered back, "Don't worry about it! It happens. Besides, Lucas only wants to read books about fans, and there really aren't any, so it's all good!"

As I drove home, I thought, "You know, she's right." I've only been able to find one book about a kid who loves fans, which another mom created by compiling pictures of her son and various fans. It's cute and we have a copy. Beyond that, there really aren't any books about fans. Believe me, I had looked everywhere. At the house, I sat down in front of my laptop and wrote out a little rhyming story based on a song I'd made up for Lucas about fans. It went like this:

Fans, fans everywhere

Spinning so fast they're blowin' my hair

Fans over here and fans over there

At the fans I love to stare

Fans are FAN-tastic! Fans are FAN-tastic!

I took this song, typed it out, built upon it and thought, "I may have something here!" and announced in a Facebook post that I was looking for an illustrator. People responded immediately and I zeroed in on one girl in particular whose portfolio featured several images of Harry Potter characters, which was a huge attraction for me. Next, I found an editor, publisher and printer, and long story short, a year later *Fans Are Fantastic* by Carrie Fabris, beautifully illustrated by Hannah Eckhardt, came to life. 500 books went to Amazon and 1,500 were delivered to my front porch.

Writing that book was one of my greatest accomplishments. Not only did it put the biggest smile on my son's face, I donated some of the proceeds to special-needs charities and it felt good. Sometimes, when your kid loves something that may seem odd, you just have to lean in. What's even more amazing is that literally all of our friends know about Lucas and his love of fans. Over the years, Andres and I have received many text messages "for Lucas" from various friends and family with videos and pictures of fans they see out and about. It's the best. Talk about leaning in!

When your kid loves something that may seem odd, you just have to lean in.

My son has taught me more lessons than anyone or anything in my life. He has taught me not to take things so seriously, and how to self-regulate quickly when I'm about to explode with frustration, and how to see things that might otherwise go unnoticed (like a fan spinning over my head on high speed). He has taught me how to genuinely laugh, especially when he comes flying into a room out of nowhere, pauses, looks at me seriously, and simply says "incoming!" That's his way of telling me I'm about to get attacked with kisses. I'll take it any day of the week.

Miss Glitter Sparkles

My girl, Lala, sees everything through glittery, sparkly lenses. She is a nurturing empath, full of positivity, the peacekeeper in our family, lover of all things magic, with a strategic mind, and is a quick study.

Fiercely passionate about dressing up and putting on a show in our living room—to which an actual ticket must be acquired, and seats taken before the show will begin—Lala is the queen of the microphone and a master with the dance moves. When she was three years old, we did a karaoke duo to Justin Timberlake's "Can't Stop the Feeling" and I'm pretty sure it broke the Internet when Andres posted it on Facebook. With the mic to her mouth and fist in the air, Lala insisted, "I'm the star! I'm the STAR!" And she totally was!

One time, she had a play date with a friend, the memory of which lasted long after the other little girl went home. While I worked upstairs, I left them un-chaperoned (my first mistake) making an art project with glitter (my second mistake). I came downstairs and found them decorating pictures on the floor of the entry hall and quickly lost my mind! This "glitter freaking everywhere" project would have been too easy on the kitchen table over newspaper. No, this had to be done on the floor where glitter loves to cling, forever.

Mid-mom-tirade, Lala looked up at me, sweetly smiling and said, "Come on, everything can be made better with glitter, Mommy!" At that moment, it was like a tunnel vision or time stood still: I'm not sure which. I do remember thinking, "You know what? It sure can. My 'sweating the small stuff' attitude could be made much better with glitter, and sparkles and bling."

Everything can be made better with glitter, Mommy!

For weeks, hundreds of tiny pieces of glitter lived in our entryway, despite how many times it was swept or mopped. Each time a tiny sparkle caught my eye, I took a deep breath, slowed down, and smiled. I told myself the glitter remnants made the floor look pretty versus boring old brown hardwood, and thought of Lala's remark. Indeed, *everything can be made better with glitter.*

Lala may never truly know how many times she has saved me. When life gets hard and the mom anxiety kicks in, she's always the one to find me when I'm hiding in the bathroom crying, wipe away my tears, give me a huge hug and calm me down. It's Lala's nature to assume the role of the nurturer, not the one who needs to be nurtured. I have oftentimes felt guilty when she finds me on these occasions because I don't ever want her to feel like she has to take care of me. I also don't want her to feel scared by my emotional state. But then I reframe my thoughts and think it's not necessarily a bad thing; I'm showing her that moms cry sometimes, and it's okay. The struggle is real, baby girl. Sometimes, being a mom is rewarding and excruciating at the same time. I always remind her that there will be moments when not being strong is, in fact, a strength. Regardless, when I am feeling low, she always has a way of filling my juice tank.

It's always been very difficult to say "no" to Lala because I get the most precious "yay" from her when I say "yes." I'll never forget dropping her off for her first sleep away camp experience at Sky Ranch in Van, Texas. Initially, she was what she calls "scare-cited"—scared and excited simultaneously. After her trunk was delivered to her cabin, the reality that I was leaving, and she would have no communication with me for the next six days kicked in. Her "scare" intensified, the "cited" left the scene, and "anger" showed up ready to rumble.

I'd never seen my daughter so intensely adamant about telling me what I was going to do and what she was not going to do! "You are not leaving me here, and I am not staying!" She grabbed my hand, virtually steering me away from her cabin, and could have cared less that her belongings and beloved stuffed rabbit, BunBun were being left behind. Lala was hell bent on getting away from that camp as fast as she could, and insistent that I go along with it.

I stopped us both in our tracks, got down on a knee to be on her eye level, and calmly said, "Baby girl, remember what Taylor Swift says? 'You need to calm down. You're being too loud.' You are staying. In this state, you cannot see the amazing time you are about to have. When I come back to pick you up next Saturday, you're going to demand to come back next summer. I understand you're upset but I need you to trust me on this, and go have the time of your life."

I didn't get the precious "yay" I loved to hear so much. Instead, I got more anger and more tears. Her separation anxiety over being left at camp made her past preschool drop-offs look like a walk in the park. This was 10 times worse. Her counselor was watching this scene unfold and when I shot her a pleading "for the love of all that's holy, come help me!" look, she rushed over. The counselor kindly tried to cheer my daughter up and steered her back into the cabin to get her bunk set up.

Before she rounded the corner, Lala instructed me to, "Stay right here!" I said, "I will stay here for a little bit and then I'm going. I love you. Have a blast." The minute she was out of sight, I turned and ran as fast as I could away from the cabin. All the other parents who had witnessed the entire showdown were laughing and cheering me on.

Of course, when I picked her up a week later, I swooped her up into a solid, three-minute hug and asked the anticipated question, "So, did you have a great time? Do you think you want to come back next summer?" I waited for the anticipated answer. She gave me the side "duh, Mom" look, and replied with a strong "YES!" I smiled, and in my head, I said "yay."

My daughter has taught me to see the sparkle and joy in everyday life, glitter or no glitter. She gets her sass from me, and her positivity from her daddy. We have our little rituals like pinky promises and a huggy-kissy-snuggly routine every night before bed. She is amazingly curious, loves to explore and the older she gets, the more I see an introversion in her that surprises me. She is fiercely loyal to her friends and a totally crazy, silly goose with her tribe. Beyond that, she is more reserved, shy at times unless a stage or microphone is nearby, and she's always watching. She reminds me that "everything is figure-out-able" (just like Marie Forleo says in the title of her amazing book), and that life is simply fun. There is always something to be happy about, to be grateful for, and when we slow down and actually look, we can see that life sparkles, just like my precious, amazing, brilliant daughter. To think I was terrified to birth this human years ago is baffling to me now. She is the light of my life.

When we slow down and actually look, we can see that life sparkles, just like my precious, amazing, brilliant daughter.

On this wild journey called being a mom, it's so interesting to unconditionally love multiple humans who show you various unpredictable facets of life, oftentimes very different from the other. Whereas my kids look alike and had almost identical sonogram pictures, they are total opposites.

Lucas is inquisitive, often distracted. He's water; he's an engineer, and a learning different kid on his own educational trajectory. Lala is strategic, often dramatic. She's fire; she's an artist, in the talented and gifted program at school, and wants to follow in her daddy's footsteps to Harvard.

As their mom, I get to experience their extremes, their passions, their likenesses, and their differences. Whereas my husband is focused on the individual when it comes to fairness, I tend to lean towards equality, and it's tricky to be the mom in the middle sometimes. So, I'm constantly ensuring that I give both kiddos equal time, attention, love and the occasional toy just for the hell of it.

They teach me how to love, how to navigate emotions beyond my own, how to show up for them, and how to see life through their eyes. They teach me that it's okay (and damn-near necessary) to show real and raw feelings, and that having boundaries is healthy for all of us. They teach me that they want to know me, they show me that they understand I have a career that I love, and they are more than happy to belt out Queen songs with me at any given moment.

They are the reason I must put myself first, refill the tank, and play all out for them as often as possible. The truth is that without these two humans coming into my life, choosing me and saving me, I might not have ever had the opportunity or courage to go through the transition that I did. They gave me a reason to put myself first in order to show up and be the mom for them that they deserve. After all, part of my transition was putting the lessons that they were teaching me into practice. These two showed me why having a livelier, juicier life was so important, for not only myself but for my family as well. Happy mama—no drama. #blessed.

Pupper Nugget

In March of 2020, my family suffered a devastating loss. Well, it was devastating for me. Our 15-year-old Lhasa Apso, Oliver, also known as Pupper, crossed the rainbow bridge. Whereas he was old, losing his hearing and eyesight, and starting to suffer from kidney disease, I was not ready for him to go. Pupper was staying with my dad at his farm, something he did on many occasions, because we were getting ready to go out of town for spring break. Dad loved having Pupper come stay with him and his little dog, Snickers, and referred to the happy trio as "three mutts at the farm."

Right before we left for our trip, my dad called. I could tell he was trying to tell me something and having a hard time finding the words. Finally, he said, "Pupper's gone." In utter disbelief, I said, "What do you mean he's gone?" Dad said, "Well, he…he died," and I lost it. Crying uncontrollably, not believing what I was hearing, I struggled to utter those same words back to him. "He died? Oh my god! What happened?" Then Dad started crying, too. I don't think anyone loved that dog as much as I did except my dad. He painstakingly recounted Pupper's final hours on this earth, the details of which aren't terribly important. Personally, I think Pupper was ready to go. He always wanted to be a farm dog, he died in a place he loved, and he will rest there on the farm for all of eternity.

I knew what to do when I lost a person I loved. Lord knows, I'd had enough practice but losing my dog was next level. That furball gave me such joy and comfort (he was a master cuddler). I "inherited" him from my friend Gina when she moved to San Francisco. First, we started looking after him for a few weeks so she could get settled. A few weeks turned into a few months, and by then, I was a goner. This dog had stolen my heart—hook, line, and sinker. I couldn't even fathom returning him.

As fate would once again have it, Oliver and I were meant to be. Gina was busy with her new job and couldn't give him the time or attention he needed. She asked if I could keep him at the very moment I was about to ask her if I could. It was perfect! She knew he had landed in a loving home and I didn't have to face the unimaginable sadness of letting him go. And for the next 13 years, Oliver Titus Fabris was by my side, patient, kind and the best dog on the planet.

After he passed away, I needed time to mourn and a break from having a pet. A few months after Oliver died, I got a text from Gina. There was nothing in the message but a link to Austin Goldendoodles. "Uh, oh," I thought, "here we go again." I called her right away to see what she was up to, and she said her family had just put a deposit down for one of the puppies from the site. They were pretty damn cute, I had to admit, but was I ready to go down the path of dog love again?

In one sentence, I went from saying, "There is no way in holy hell we're spending $3,000 on a dog," to "Who do I call to put down a nonrefundable deposit?" Andres agreed that we were all ready, especially the kids. They loved Oliver, but he was always primarily my dog. Lucas, in particular, said he wanted a "big, jumpy dog." I contacted the breeder, put down a deposit, and we were twelfth on the waiting list.

In October, a litter of nine pups was born: eight boys and one girl. I wanted a boy because I am a boy dog mom, and planned to keep it that way. As much as I wanted to surprise the kids with a Christmas puppy, we were too far down the waiting list to get a puppy from the October litter. But I scrolled the breeder's Instagram page on a daily basis anyway to track the puppy's progress and wallow in their cuteness. One of the pups—she called him Green Bow Boy—was a precious thing with a little white dash on his nose. My disappointment in not getting one of these sweet babies RIGHT NOW was growing.

Then, one day in early December, I got a text from the breeder. "Hello! One of the puppies is available. Do you want him?" I was totally confused. How is this even possible? Surprised and ecstatic, I asked her to send me a picture of him. It was Green Bow Boy! I couldn't believe it! Yes, we wanted him!

We arranged to meet in a Kohl's parking lot in Austin the following Friday. Like a drug deal I imagine, I drove the three hours from Dallas, Venmo'd her $3000, she handed the puppy over, the deal was done and she drove off. I stood there in the parking lot holding my new mini Goldendoodle baby as he licked my face and nose. The puppy breath was divine; a better score than any drug imaginable.

I drove him home while he barked in his crate most of the way. Andres and I had a plan. I pulled into the garage, he came out to get the puppy, and put him in a large box in the living room. Meanwhile, I went upstairs to say hi to the kids and keep them distracted. Like clockwork, Andres gave me the all-clear and the kids went running downstairs to open their early Christmas present. When they saw the large box, they were baffled. Together, they busted the box open and were speechless with shock when they saw the cutest puppy face looking up at them.

"Merry Christmas!" Andres and I yelled in unison. Lala instantly started cuddling him. "Who is this little precious thing!?" Lucas was jumping up and down yelling, "Oh my god! Can we keep him? Is he ours?" Andres and I were beaming.

Before bringing the new puppy home, we had started a list of names for him. Andres wanted to name him Lenny (a tribute to Lenny Kravitz). I wanted to name him Dash for that little dash of white on his nose. When Lala picked him up and snuggled with him, she lovingly referred to him as Nugget. Andres and I looked at each other and said, "Well, that's a pretty good name. Nugget it is!"

Nugget Nibbler Nicholas Bourbon Fabris was the pup we had been waiting for. He has an amazing soul, eats everything in sight, which is infuriating, and is the biggest ball of love.

Dogs make us juicy too. They are always in the present and always happy to see us. Whenever you feel depleted, sad, or have any negative feelings of any kind, turn to a dog. They are amazing teachers about living in the moment and loving everything about life and those around you.

Walking On Sunshine

Today, I'm a very different person than the Carrie I was when I boarded that flight to London in 2016. On this side of my journey, it's sometimes remarkable to me that I actively chose to go through all I did to find fulfillment and live a juicy life. Things that seemed painfully hard back then are now daily "normal" practices such as acknowledging fear when it shows up and welcoming it in. I know it's there to tell me what I need to learn versus choosing to cower in the corner frozen and terrified. Speaking of frozen, when I hear "Show Yourself" from *Frozen 2* now, I damn-near search for a mic so I can belt it out, confident that I have stepped into my power. I still cry a little when I hear it but my tears are from humility and joy at feeling fulfilled, not from the sadness and frustration I carried for years.

My business surpassed my initial Big Hairy Audacious Goal by miles, and it has reached a level of success that I truly never could have imagined. I outsourced my marketing initiatives to an awesome team, and with their help, CareerFrame LLC has evolved into the master brand of Carrie Fabris: speaker, author, consultant and ecourse creator.

I continue to coach high-level executives, primarily women, and work with amazing corporate clients on team dynamics, leadership, alignment, and emotional intelligence. Every engagement with me begins with a CliftonStrengths® assessment, which we build off of to ensure badassery is reached, personally and professionally. I'm a tough love coach, and as an activator, I get impatient with inaction. I show up for my clients and therefore I expect them to show up for themselves.

My new mission in life is to inspire others to claim their power, lean into their strengths, and unapologetically choose themselves first so they can then show up for others from a place of love. My hope, especially for working moms, is that we all create juicy lives that serve as inspiration to our children, our daughters in particular. When we identify our purpose, do the work to bring it to life, and follow our hearts, we will win every time, even when things get challenging. If we embrace uncertainty and focus on what we can control, we can't help but live a juiced-up life.

My new mission in life is to inspire others to claim their power, lean into their strengths, and unapologetically choose themselves first so they can then show up for others from a place of love.

I choose to enjoy life within reason. Clearly, as well documented, I've yo-

yoed between paying off debt and racking up more. But I'm humble as shit because after being in debt for over a decade, I don't take the income I have now for granted. The light at the end of the debt tunnel is shining big and bright where once there was only darkness. My journey back to my business and doing what I love has helped Andres and me pay the debt down to where now it's a tiny annoyance versus the haunting mountain it used to be. We have a financial plan of being debt-free in the very near future and we're still enjoying life to the fullest.

As for the financial infidelity Andres accused me of when I stubbornly decided to go all in on my transformation journey, well, no one has been in more awe, more supportive and prouder of who I have become than him. He still stands by the accusation but he fully understands why I had to make a choice for myself, so I could show up for him and for Lucas and Lala. They were my why then, and they are my why now; they always will be.

Find Your Juicy Life

Celebrate unique gifts and perspectives.
The beauty of humanity is that we are all, each one of us, unique. Each of us has gifts that no one else has, and when we have people in our lives that are different, we need to celebrate them. Lean in to minds that think differently, seek to understand them, and appreciate the lens through which they see the world. You might learn a beautiful thing or two.

Don't sweat the small stuff.
The best thing you can do for yourself is focus on what you can control and let go of all the other stuff you can't. As Marie Forleo says, "Everything is figure-out-able." When we get worked up over things that are not even remotely important, and no one is dying because of it, we are simply choosing to be negative and waste energy. Don't do that. Don't worry about the little gnats in your face. Eventually they will fly away.

Welcome love bursts into your heart and home.
Partners, kids, fur babies, and the like—thank God we have these magical creatures in our lives. Welcome the lessons they teach you and show your love by listening to those lessons.

Reflect on joyous accomplishments.
Focus on what you are doing right versus what you are doing wrong. This is what CliftonStrengths® is all about. We get so caught up in where we need to improve that we don't reflect on where we kick ass. Celebrate your accomplishments, and celebrate loud!

Lessons Learned through Fulfillment

Stepping into my professional potential to focus on CareerFrame full time was years in the making. I learned, with a front row seat, that change takes time. I gave myself the time and space to explore what felt right for me. I learned that each of us is on our own journey and therefore, it will unfold on our own timeline. Give yourself at least 12 months to create massive change in your life and do not beat yourself up if it takes longer. While the 12 months of 2019 was when I had the most transformation, I'm still growing and evolving every day. The key is to keep going and to not give up. We all have responsibilities that can get in the way of our dreams and passions but when our heart is calling, we must listen. Your heart will never steer you wrong, even if it takes years to see it and admit it.

Once I finally made the decision to leave my corporate job, no matter what, and go all in on my own soul path, I had to continue to invest in the support systems that would allow me to succeed. I had to continue to examine the emotions and the mindsets that held me back. I had to swallow my poisonous pride, admit my shortcomings out loud, ask for forgiveness, and own the past to embrace the future.

Though my goal was CareerFrame Island, I was not an island, and there is a small army of people who helped me set the course to get there. My quest for a juicy life demanded nothing less than unapologetic conviction and the humility to seek and ask for help.

If the pandemic and lockdown taught me anything, it taught me that perspective can make or break a seemingly untenable situation. Like most families, mine was initially unmoored until we found a groove, which involved a tidal wave of emotions, trial and error, and patience.

It is surreal to witness the success I've enjoyed since stepping into my purpose and following my heart. I'm in shock and awe every day that I made the brave decision to sort some massive shit out, find coaches, gurus, and mentors, stop shaming myself over debt and give myself permission to do what I loved. My journey from frustrated to fulfilled was packed with lessons both simple and profound: lean in, breathe, take your time, trust, keep going and watch how the universe rewards you when you step up and go all in.

CONCLUSION

PERMISSION TO BE UNAPOLOGETIC

> "You are responsible for what you say and do. You are not responsible for whether or not people freak out about it."
> –Jen Sincero, *You Are A Badass*

As I look back over the years of my personal and professional transformation as a working mom, I realize that a large part of my success was as a result of giving myself permission to do what I needed to do, unapologetically. I didn't wait for approval from my husband, kids, family or friends to do some of the things that my heart was screaming at me to do. As uncomfortable as some of these decisions were for them, and at times for me, they were a necessary means to a powerful and meaningful end.

Some people might say that some of my choices were self-centered. And yes, some of them were. Some people might say I lacked empathy for others. Occasionally, I did and some days, I still do. My goal was never to—nor ever will be to—be bitchy, thoughtless or cold-hearted. My perceived lack of empathy is due to decades of trauma. I simply do not have the capacity to take on other people's pain, as I've had enough of my own to last a few lifetimes. There are some decisions in life that have to be made for ourselves. And there are times that demand we must be centered on ourselves before we can show up for others.

Each of us must determine how we define being unapologetic for ourselves. My story is about how I defined it, for me, in my circumstances. It's about how the choices I made impacted me, sometimes at the risk of them impacting others. When those around us are impacted, of course, we want to make sure they are not impacted negatively. But we also need to realize that sometimes when those around us *react* negatively, it's because they can't or won't see how our actions will lead to a positive effect down the road.

Unfortunately, when we decide we want to grow or change, sometimes those around us are the first to try to talk us out of it. Perhaps we will change in a direction they don't like or can't relate to. Perhaps by taking actions for ourselves we hold a mirror up that reflects the actions they are not initiating for themselves, and this can be very uncomfortable. Often, in the face of extreme—or even subtle—change, relationships are tested, and we grow apart.

Giving ourselves permission to unapologetically do what our heart needs is hard.

It can even be excruciating, and cause massive guilt, because we're conditioned to serve everyone else first. We are all 100 percent responsible for ourselves, and we can only control ourselves: what we do, say, feel, and think.

Take immensely good care of yourself. This one was a hard one for me, but it got easier over time. My guilty pleasure is the infrared sauna. I enjoy the heat and detox almost daily. I get a massage once or twice a month because, well, why the hell not? I work out and I drink wine. Every year, I find a coach who will help me work through something heavy on my mind. First, it was Molly; then it was my Results coach Jenn; then it was Lou, my mentor and strategic advisor; and I will continue to seek others as I move forward. I am committed to investing in my growth and development every year, and some years are more financially demanding than others. I know that an investment of any kind in myself will get the greatest ROI.

The frustrated and stressed-out woman on that first-class flight to London had no idea that in five years, she would become a fulfilled career woman and mom living in accordance with her soul path. Once I gave myself permission to go on that trip, disconnect from my adorable kids, and juice myself up by claiming treasured alone time, I set my transformational journey in motion.

Writing this book has been an instrumental part of that journey. Whereas I did the bulk of my personal work with Molly, the work continues each day. Writing my story was a profound way to remind myself of what I went through and the emotions I felt along the way. It reiterated the importance of that work and served as a reminder that I must continue to live my best, juiced-up life and remain fulfilled. I share this story with my sisters in arms, all the moms out there, with the intention to inspire them to choose themselves. We moms deserve a daily medal for all that we do, and the most rewarding medal we receive is the one we give to ourselves.

My hope is that I am an example of an ordinary woman who realized I wanted more. I felt something was getting in my way and got curious to find out what it was by seeking support, taking action, and doing the hard work. I gave myself the space and time to declutter my mind, listen to my heart, and make shit happen on my way to a happy, juicy life. Sure, I still have my moments where I shit, fuck, damn and bitch my way through the ups and downs. But now, I reframe the situation. I'm able to see potential in my frustration because, after all, it means a breakthrough is coming and that's exciting.

At the risk of sounding cliché, anything is possible. Anything! Everything is infinite. I have embraced the idea that when something is lost, something else is found. When something ends, something else begins. When something dies, something else is born, and it is all guided by divine timing.

We all must stop trying to control the outcome of everything. We can only ever hope to control ourselves, and we must take care of ourselves before we can serve others. So put your own oxygen mask on first. Tony Robbins says, "Life will pay you whatever price you ask of it." Aim high and ask for it all. Go all in. Make your life livelier and fuller. Make it unapologetically juicy.

- THE END -

AFTERWORD

A SALUTE TO MOMS WHO GO ALL IN

Most of us moms will do pretty much anything for our kids. So much so, that we put ourselves last, take on heavy burdens, and go through hell and back to ensure their safety, health and happiness. As my transformation journey unfolded, I was fortunate enough to hear stories of other moms who have gone through the fires of fear, uncertainty, or plain old life circumstances to emerge juicier, livelier, and all-around more fulfilled.

Some say they are still a work in progress. Really, aren't we all in some capacity? In support and solidarity of the collective mom challenges, some of those brave women have graciously agreed to share their stories here. They exemplify the concept that no matter your personal circumstances, going all in on yourself will always be the best path to an unapologetically juicy life. These six women bravely recall the precise moments that their lives shifted into focus, when they realized that putting themselves first was the only way to be their best selves, so they could show up in true mom-style for everyone else. And like me, their kids were at the center of their why. Here are their amazing stories.

Purpose-Driven Nomad by Laura Helen

Laura and I met in a Zoom breakout room during a Tony Robbins seminar. She was part of the Crew for the event, and the timing of her appearance in my life was no coincidence. As a matter of fact, she pulled this entire book out of me when I hired her to be my ideation coach.

Originally from the United Kingdom, Laura and her family are living their best nomad life, often relocating to different cities and countries around the world. Their lives certainly didn't start out that way.

In the early days of their marriage, Laura and her husband were living in a cottage by the beach. They had steady jobs, a year's salary in savings and a baby on the way. Out of the blue, a family member mentioned a couple that had a 3-year-old daughter who they were unable to manage. The little girl was nonverbal, and the mother and her boyfriend were at their wit's end. With a huge belly and very little energy, Laura had "no hesitation to take the girl in for a few days to give everyone a break." When the few days were up and it was time to go home, the child appeared terrified, and all emotional hell broke loose. Assuming the outburst was related to the child's developmental challenges, Laura gave her a hug and left.

A few days later, the couple reached out with a troubling offer. Did Laura want to keep the child? Because if not, they were going to drop her off somewhere else and move on with their lives. Again, without hesitation, Laura Helen and her husband took the child in. Under their care, the girl started to slowly share bits and pieces of the horrific abuse she had suffered at the hands of her own mother and the mother's boyfriend. When word spread within the child's family of the situation, the grandparents and the biological father suddenly came out of the woodwork to get involved. None of them followed through on their promises and Laura quickly went into action to build a team of attorneys and adopt the little girl.

What followed was a two-year legal battle, early into which Laura gave birth to a son. She had to stop working to care for her newborn and the little girl, as well as oversee the adoption case. She and her husband went from a stable, dual income lifestyle with money in the bank to a low-paying, single income, a massive five-figure debt, and two kids. To add insult to injury, the girl's mother and her boyfriend walked away free and clear of any financial or legal responsibility. The girl was the only witness to what had happened to her, and she was too traumatized to speak about it. Laura didn't want to force her, so no charges were ever pressed.

One day, Laura dropped her husband off at work. They were flat broke. They'd had to sell off household possessions simply to put food on the table, and the car was on empty. She couldn't afford gas money to get home, and it was four degrees outside. She asked her husband to run inside and borrow £20 from a co-worker.

When he handed her the borrowed bill, the gravity of the situation came crashing down on her. How had their lives taken this trajectory when all they wanted to do was save and love a child from an unhealthy home? She told me, "At that moment, I felt like I had failed as a person, as a mom and as a partner. I was mad at the world and blamed all the external factors. I thought, 'This all has to stop right now.'"

She got gas, pulled up her big girl pants, went home and made a plan. She was good at selling their own possessions for cash, so she started buying items on Amazon and selling them for a markup on Ebay. She joined an MLM business, started blogging, gaining followers and building a community. Then she watched one of Tony Robbins' interventions with a traumatized 30-year-old woman online and realized, "I must get my daughter this help NOW; not in 20 or 30 years. I can't let her carry this pain for her whole life."

Laura told me, "We were so close to losing everything, but I had a strong intuition about the possibility of what we could gain. Instead of paying rent that month, we bought a ticket for me to attend *Unleash the Power Within*. I was scared shitless—but we took the risk."

A year later, Laura's daughter had found her voice. She had even written a few children's books, which landed in Tony Robbins' hands. Laura took the whole family to the next UPW, and Tony invited them all backstage. He told her to "keep going"; he said she was "an outstanding mom." He also invited them to *Date with Destiny* as his personal guest. Laura said that Tony's words and generosity "knocked all the self-doubt out of me." After the event, Laura realized she had to BE her best self to show up as her best self for her family. She set up a morning routine of priming, jumping on the rebounder and ice plunge baths. She went all in and lost 56 pounds. Her family watched in awe, and eventually, joined her.

Laura and her husband created a business to help people "create their life by design" through writing books. The more she showed up "as if" to her community, the more her passion came through and the more clients they got. She focused mainly on people in the U.S., so she could be a mom during the day and work at night. They were on their way but they were still drowning in debt and had to cut expenses. When Laura discovered AirBNB, she and her family condensed their four-bedroom house into four carry-on suitcases. They sold or donated everything they owned, and started living from AirBNB to AirBNB, "jumping without parachutes" every step of the way.

For the next several years, they lived in London, Las Vegas, Los Angeles, Utah, Miami, Costa Rica, Paris, Spain and Romania...to name a few. They started exploring extended house-sitting opportunities and now, when they move around, they have no rent or bills to pay. Laura "unschools" her kids, teaching them through life experiences. Both of her children have written 25 books in three languages and the whole family writes, creates, speaks and lives. They are debt-free, loving their business at booksboostbusiness.co.uk/ and sharing their journey at foreverfamilyforeverfree.com.

Showing Up Stronger by Danielle

When I met Danielle through a mutual friend, she was working through decades of deep-seeded trauma. As a single mom with a teenage son, she knew she had to get past it.

Danielle suffered abuse in one form or another since she was 2 years old. Her mother's abuse was physical, her father's was verbal (suggesting that women are only good for one thing), and her uncle's was sexual. She coped with it all the best she could. When she was 24, she was drugged and raped by a business associate of her father's.

Despite what she had endured, Danielle obtained a master's degree and established a successful career in sales and marketing. She also dabbled in drugs and alcohol and had a tendency to get involved with the wrong kind of men. In her mid-30s, she was living in the Northeast and had a steady career when she got pregnant. When the guy found out, he fled. Her mother died two months before her son was born. After giving birth, all her past trauma rose to the surface. To get away from her toxic family and be around supportive friends, she and her son moved out West.

Four years later, she met a man who swept her off her feet. He convinced her to marry him and move to the Mid-Atlantic. Danielle had a successful job, bought a beautiful home for their family, and protected it with a pre-nup. It was revealed that her new husband was a covert operations specialist. In addition to his training in manipulation, he suffered from narcissistic personality disorder and complex PTSD.

He successfully convinced her that *she* was the crazy one, isolated her from her friends, and talked her into going to one of his doctors who loaded her up on a prescription medication cocktail. "Every antidepressant out there, I was on it," she told me. "And I couldn't sleep, so the doctor added Ambien to the mix. The reason I couldn't sleep is because my husband banged on the pipes in the basement. When I finally passed out from exhaustion, he would rape me."

Danielle felt numb, in a constant mind fog. She had to give up her full-time job and take on a part-time consulting role instead. In the depths of her hellish ordeal, she managed to find an inkling of strength and told her husband she wanted to separate. This was met with further abuse and retaliation. Desperate, she reached out to her small group of female friends, from whom she'd been isolated, for support. With their help, she found a therapist, who validated the abuse and trauma, and made a plan to wean off the pills.

Somehow, she convinced her husband to attend a 30-day, and then 60-day, program for covert narcissism, which bought her some breathing room and relief. More importantly, while he was away, she noticed a significant change in her son. He was more relaxed, less anxious, and a lot less argumentative with her. All along, she had been consumed with her own state, but now, with a clearer head, she saw how much he had suffered too. This was bigger than her, and she knew her husband could not come back. She told him it was over, for good this time, and he insisted on coming back immediately. Filled with fear, Danielle flew into action. Within 24 hours, she put everything they had in storage and went to a safe house basement apartment where she and her son would be protected.

One day, while her son was at school, she hit rock bottom. She said, "There, in that basement, I was at the end of the couch, in a fetal position, bawling. I looked around at the mousetrap in the corner and the muddy footprints on the floor from the dog, consumed with a smell of boiling cabbage from upstairs, trying to not vomit. I felt the damage from all of the medication on my brain and sat there in a total shame storm, baffled at how I let myself get to this place. I felt like I was failing at life, failing as a mom, and I was suicidal. That's when I made a decision. I was going to double down and put every resource into me: for me and for my son."

With a friend, Danielle attended an event where she heard a woman share her personal and powerful story of triumph in the face of adversity. She reached out to the woman and a dear friendship was ignited, which led to the woman gifting her three months of sessions with a coach she had worked with and trusted. Danielle decided to get rid of her therapist and focus on the coaching exclusively. She stopped drinking and taking the rest of the medications she was on. Every now and then, a bottle of wine found its way to her lips but now, she was able to recognize why it was happening and quickly rebound. Most noticeably, she was able to cry and shed her emotions, whereas before she was only able to numb. She embraced exercise and invited friends on daily walks to help keep her mind focused.

Feeling stronger, she officially filed for divorce and started looking for a home. Through divine intervention in an impossible real estate market and still without a job, she found a house to rent in a family-friendly neighborhood, close to a great school for her son. She continued to create a foundation of healing through her coach and by practicing Reiki and meditation. A new doctor gave her a thoughtful diagnosis and prescribed her Trintellix, an anti-depressant, anti-anxiety medication that has helped her immensely.

"Nothing has been linear on this journey. I've been up, down, this way, sideways, upside down. The consistent comfort has been the supportive group of women around me and finding my best self so I can be there for my son and be the mom he needs me to be. As I worked through the trauma, I started sleeping. Then, as the anxiety oozed away, confidence showed up, my reactions were not so intense, my mental fog lifted, and now I can be in the present. I went from 115 pounds at five-feet-eight to a healthier 130."

A year later, the divorce was finalized, and the house was sold. Now, she has money in the bank and just landed THE dream job at a top technology company. Danielle and her son are thriving. She remarks, "Just a year ago, it was a struggle to drive across town to the grocery store." Instead, last summer, she and her son went on a volunteer trip to South America. She says, "I still have a way to go but I am able to 'show up' now, stronger than I've ever been. And I'm going to keep going!"

Leaning In by Rian

I met Rian in a swimming pool in Cabo San Lucas. Seeing the similarities in our families—white girl mom, Hispanic dad, older son and younger daughter, I swam over and said hello. They were from Virginia, loved Mexico, and had always wanted to move somewhere warm and Spanish-speaking, yet the timing was never right. Rian was a branding badass but there was a sadness about her.

She and her family were on this particular vacation to try to heal from a devastating loss. They had been fostering a 5-year-old girl from Guatemala. It was suggested she could end up being with them forever because her biological family's whereabouts were unknown. They all felt an instant love and connection to the child, and after several months, had settled as a new, expanded family. Then, the foster agency called and informed them that the little girl's mother had been found and they needed to be reunited immediately. With zero time to emotionally prepare the kids, the agency came to remove the little girl from their home at 2 a.m. Whereas she knew it was the right thing for the little girl and her mother, Rian fell into a devastating depression. This trip to Mexico was meant to be an escape from their sadness and chance to find solace in the sun. It only reinforced their desire to want to move somewhere warm and Spanish-speaking.

Back home, Rian and her family fostered another child, a teenage boy. As an empath, she accepted the placement without many details and quickly discovered he had many layers of trauma. Caring for the boy added more delays to the family's desire to leave Virginia. In the peak of Covid, her two children and foster child were struggling with online school and the isolation that came with it. Her foster son started demonstrating behaviors that frightened Rian and her husband. She knew something had to change.

Putting the warm weather and Spanish-speaking requirements aside, Rian and her husband started looking for "local" places to move. They went to Wilmington for a weekend and knew instantly it was not where they were supposed to be. Then they went to Charleston. That wasn't it either. Then they drove to Florida. Nope. On the drive back to Virginia, Rian brought up Cabo. Why couldn't they move there? Why did it seem so out of reach?

The more they spoke about it, the more they could imagine the possibilities. Back home, Rian called her business partner. He had been her professor and mentor in grad school, many years before he asked her to start an innovative branding agency of their own. Two years after they started the business together, she posed the idea of Cabo, fully expecting push back because why on earth would this dream come true? To her immediate disbelief, he was 1000 percent behind it. And he reminded her that the company was built on the foundational belief that they should all LIVE while working. The rest of the partners backed her up, and suddenly, she told me, "the door was wide-ass open."

But first, she had to find a suitable arrangement for their foster son, who she loved but was not able to manage to the extent he needed. There was another couple in the area who specialized in helping foster boys ages 14 to 18 with severe trauma, and they agreed to step in. After a few days, it was clear that the new arrangement was a winning fit for everyone. With him beautifully taken care of, she turned her focus to the practicalities of the move.

A year after that initial beach vacation, Rian packed up her family and moved to Cabo San Lucas. With a secure income under her belt and the branding firm's full support, they sold their home and whatever didn't fit into a small trailer and drove from Virginia to Mexico. After staying in a friend's place for a couple of weeks, they found an amazing permanent home.

Rian told me, "As crazy as the plan sounded, my gut knew we were meant to be somewhere else. All of my life, I had always been a square peg in a round hole. I had a lot of trauma and loss as a little girl and yet, when I played by myself, there was always a narrative running in my head. I told myself that all of what I was going through was conditioning me for a better life, and that little girl truly wanted to believe it. And now I look up, and here I am, living the most amazing life, with amazing kids, an amazing husband, and incredible career, and I get to go to the beach everyday if I want. In my adult life, there was a lot of self-doubt. I had done a lot of self-reflection and knew what was not for me, but still, I felt like that square peg in a round hole. But the truth is, I went from being in a hole to being whole!"

With her kids thriving at an amazing international school, her business booming, and an iron-clad loving marriage, Rian is able to lean into her own self-care, and when she does, she can lean into the family she loves in a place she loves.

Becoming Human by Amanda

Amanda and I met through a mutual friend. She is a lovely, British, force of a woman who has grown into an unrecognizable and vastly improved version of her former self.

When Amanda was growing up, her parents worked constantly, to the degree that they were largely absent from her life. She was entrusted to the care of her two sisters, who didn't want her around. One of them tried to drown her in the bathtub when she was little. Their younger brother was the "cherub" of the family and the favorite. Within this dynamic, Amanda always felt out of place and often wondered if she was adopted. She felt like a burden unless she did exactly what others told her to do, even if it meant putting herself in precarious situations. At the age of 14, she was assaulted after one of her sisters drugged her.

Amanda grew up to be a people pleaser with the hope that if she pleased others, they would love her. Through her teen and young adult years, she battled deep depression and was once hospitalized for it. She told herself she wasn't good enough or worthy of love. She rarely, if ever, felt safe or secure with her immediate family.

Raised Irish Catholic, when she got married, she wanted a big family that would love her unconditionally. Things didn't quite work out as planned. After her son was born, Amanda's narrative about being unlovable reared its ugly head. She didn't trust herself and she had low self-worth. She struggled to love her husband and child wholeheartedly, but her affection was clouded by her own overwhelming desire to be loved by her mother and father, a love she would truly never receive.

As her son grew older, he learned the behaviors she was modeling. One time, Amanda asked him to get milk out of the refrigerator, and when he couldn't find it, he flew into a crying rage yelling, "It's not my fault! It's not my fault!" When she realized her son was mirroring her own wounded child, she was consumed with guilt and desperate to stop the cycle of low self-worth.

A friend told her about Anna Garcia and her Relationships Intensive program. Amanda had no understanding that the journey to a happier life even existed, but she had nothing to lose by checking it out. At the first session, she was mesmerized by the energy and found a tribe of supportive friends who gave her the space to be herself. For the first time, she was able to speak from her wounded child's heart without being judged or silenced. At one meeting, she recalls hearing the phrase "thank you, what you think of me is none of my business," which sent her into a sort of exorcism. As her brain battled to comprehend its meaning, something started to crack open.

Amanda decided to write a memoir about her experiences, and she worked hard to get her words and thoughts out on the page. When she read the final product, she felt it was "total shit—nothing but a 'woe is me' monologue." She decided she wanted nothing more to do with that person's life and narrative. She trashed the first draft and, within a week, rewrote it from a new perspective. In 2020, *I Choose Me* became a best seller in the U.K. and a key turning point in her healing journey.

Through Relationship Intensive, meditation, her tribe and releasing the childhood pain through her first memoir attempt, she shifted. She realized she had been a human "doing" all her life, not a human "being." She told me, "It's like I grew up in the last four years, from that wounded child to an empowered, fulfilled, happy adult at the age of 54. Once I was awake, I was able to see and hear the trauma-filled narrative I had been telling and selling myself for decades. I was able to see that I could heal that wounded child's heart, find her through deep meditation, and give her the motherly love that she never had. I healed her broken heart and am now living my best life in unison."

Amanda went on to write a series of books for children and parents called *The Mood Munchers*. Today, she is content: full of positive energy, madly in love with her husband and son and still writing books to help others heal. She also has a successful podcast called You Choose You Now. You can find out more about Amanda at www.amandahryall.com.

Finding Balance by Andrea

I met Andrea through a former CareerFrame client. She immediately struck me as a confident, strong, determined, ultra-high achiever.

A devoted career woman, she barely had time to be with her husband and daughter. For nine and a half years, she gave her heart and soul to the company she worked for, contributing to key products and brand initiatives. Her managers frequently came and went, some good, some bad. In 2018, she was casually told that a new, incoming manager had been informed of how "difficult she was to work with, that she lacked leadership skills, was too straightforward and was not a strong listener." It seemed that no matter how much of herself Andrea gave to the company, throwing passion at everything along the way, she was highly misunderstood at work.

Disheartened, Andrea felt like she faced an uphill battle to disprove other people's unfavorable opinions. She aimed to be perfect in the eyes of her co-workers, and her stress level grew. Her desire to be seen and appreciated at work started to consume her. It impacted her marriage to the brink of divorce, and she felt immense guilt about not being there for her teenage daughter. While she carried the weight of being the primary wage earner in her household, she began to feel overwhelmed, underappreciated, burned out and empty. She got so low, she no longer recognized who she was. She knew her life needed to improve.

In addition to getting on medication, Andrea sought out a coach and committed to a year of one-to-one monthly sessions. With her coach, she faced the feedback from her co-workers, took a hard look at herself, and dove into the work she needed to do to be understood, and most importantly, to be happy. She addressed her confusion and self-doubt about how she was showing up to others and thought carefully about how she reacted and responded to people. She got into the habit of wearing a rubber band on her wrist and snapping it before meetings as a reminder to be aware of her actions, words and behaviors. She read *High Performing Habits* by Brendon Burchard, *The Untethered Soul* by Michael Singer, *Daring Greatly* by Brené Brown and *Love Warrior* by Glennon Doyle to improve how she came across. She wanted to be exactly what her co-workers wanted her to be, even if it meant she was not being true to herself.

Then, in 2019, Andrea was dealt a major blow. She was terminated, which left her feeling blindsided and devastated. In short order, those feelings grew into anger. No one had given her specific and actionable feedback. Certainly, no one was advocating for her or had offered to coach her.

Losing the job she loved at a company that did not love her in return sparked a transformative journey of self-discovery and self-love. She prioritized finding a career and a company where she could be true to herself and accepted as such by others. This quest led her to the realization that her entire identity was her career. To salvage her disintegrating marriage, build a stronger bond with her daughter, and love herself first, that had to change. With her tail between her legs, she found the strength to network and quickly discovered many people wanted to help her.

Before she could barely blink, she was offered a great opportunity with a great company and at a much higher salary. She accepted the offer and, within six months, was promoted to VP. A year later, she found herself with a seat at the executive table reporting directly to the CEO. Today, she is responsible for nine brands and a team of 12 people. She's become a highly respected thought leader, she feels appreciated and she is able to thrive in an environment that values her. Just as importantly, she is able to coach others who are in the same situation she was in with her previous employer.

Andrea told me, "The biggest part of my transformation was losing the job I loved, where they never accepted what I had to offer. It forced me to look at who I really was and more importantly, what I really wanted out of LIFE, not just work. I noticed how far I've come by growing into a leadership role where I have to help my team members navigate the same criticism I experienced personally and directly."

Two years after she was terminated, she now has gratitude towards her former employer. Their rejection ignited her path forward. She was able to step into the truth of who she is and what she has to offer. She sees that happiness in life and a kickass career can co-exist.

Starting Over by Phoebe

My dear friend Phoebe is a fellow working mom, turned full-time mom, who returned to being a working mom, but not by choice. In 2002, she married a pilot and the couple had two children. Due to his busy flight schedule, they decided Phoebe should leave her corporate job to stay home with the kids.

Eight years into the marriage, she had a troubling dream. Her husband was naked in a room with her best friend, who thought nothing of his nudity. When she woke up, she couldn't shake the feeling that her intuition was trying to tell her something. A few days later, she found out her husband and her best friend were having an affair and promptly, understandably, lost her shit. She remembers that while she was processing the news, "My immediate sadness wasn't about my husband cheating on me. It was about the friendship I was losing with my best friend who betrayed me. I was losing the two loves of my life and it hit hard!"

Months later, after the dust settled and she was able to collect herself, she and the pilot agreed to work on saving the marriage. They went to therapy and group counseling but it was clear the pilot wasn't mentally engaged. At one session, he started crying, which Phoebe thought could be attributed to his seeing the error of his ways. It turns out, he told her, he was not crying for them; he was crying for the relationship he was going to lose with the best friend.

Phoebe recalls sitting in a chair in the living room, staring at the wall, and reflecting on her situation. Her mind went to her grandparents who, in her eyes, never exuded true love. She thought about how they were married out of convenience and obligation. Even her own parents were never very affectionate toward one another. At that pivotal moment, she made a decision. She decided that she wanted more. She wanted love, passion, wild sex, laughter, and to feel worthy of those things; she knew the pilot would never deliver.

Staring at an inevitable divorce and the care of two young children, Phoebe knew she had to get back to work. She immediately landed a job that would bring stability in the dark storm of uncertainty. As the divorce unfolded, she decided to take a year to find herself, focus on her kids, and turn her pain into strength. She booked consistent sessions with her therapist to zero in on what she wanted.

The pilot, suddenly consumed with regret, wrote her a letter begging for forgiveness and trying to win her back. Phoebe looked at her emotions as a litmus test of her new-found resilience. His letter only made her stronger and more adamant that she wanted a love that he could never give her. She listened to her gut, which told her, "Hey, he's not a bad guy, he was just unhappy, but he cannot be trusted on an emotional level." When she told him how she felt, he was quick to say that he never should have sent the letter, revoking the heartfelt words he had written, which again fueled her newfound drive for happiness.

As the year progressed, she made new friends and one of them introduced her to an interesting guy. Phoebe knew she was ready to take the plunge back into dating. From there, her confidence grew along with her desire to look and feel sexy. She went out with guys she met at bars, guys she met at restaurants, and she ventured into online dating, which was a big step for her. She knew what she wanted this time, and she was not going to settle, keep quiet or adapt.

While she was dating several different men, she met Henry online. Henry stuck out from the rest. He was handsome, clever, thoughtful, made her laugh and supported her in every way. To top it off, he made her feel sexy and desired. And he was amazing in bed. As they quickly got to know each other better, Phoebe ditched the other guys she was dating.

When she finally introduced Henry to her kids, who she was thoughtfully protective of, she witnessed an instant connection amongst them. They had been through a lot with the divorce compounded by the fact that one of her children suffers from anxiety and the other was diagnosed with ADHD. Henry leaned into her kids and, just when she thought he couldn't get any more wonderful, he fully embraced their challenges and showed them that he loved them just the way they were.

As the relationship with Henry evolved, Phoebe felt more comfortable in her own skin, spoke her mind without hesitation, and most importantly, she felt empowered. It certainly helped that Henry got out of her way and let her be how she wanted to be. Years into dating, she told me, "One night we were watching a fucking romcom and it hit me. 'I have that now! I'm living my own romcom!'" On the seven-year anniversary of their first date, Phoebe and Henry got married.

Phoebe had to lose her marriage and her best friend to realize that she was not putting herself first. Sitting in that chair in the living room all those years earlier, she decided to unapologetically put her own oxygen mask on first. She gave herself the time to grow emotionally and focus on her kids' needs, without asking anyone's permission to juice up her life, juicy sex and all.

Parting Words

We women are in this together, especially us working moms. We ALL have our stories from the past, and we ALL have the power to write new ones—stories that are empowering, that help us to grow and step into the juicy lives we are supposed to live. We are all on a quest for our own version of that juicy life. Go all in and claim yours: for your babies, for your family and most of all, for you.

ACKNOWLEDGEMENTS

This book and my quest for a juicy life would not have been possible without the cast of amazing characters who contributed, supported, showed immense patience and compassion, and cheered me on along the way.

First, my A.L.L.—Andres, Lucas, and Lala. You three are my world and why I choose to show up daily as your wife and mom and as someone you can be proud of. I love you three like no other humans on this planet.

To Jessica, who told me for years to write my story. Thank you for the encouragement, for challenging me to be better and bigger, and for your endearing friendship. To Laura Helen, who pulled this story out of me when I was resisting to tell it. You coached the coach on what she needed to hear and I thank you. To Brooke, developmental editor writing coach extraordinaire, thank you for your partnership in bringing this book to life. You took what I wrote and made it into the flowing, impactful story it is today. Your 'keep it real' and tell me what I needed to hear style was exactly what I indeed needed and choosing you to partner with me on this journey was one of the best decisions ever! Thank YOU for going "all in" with me on this journey. To Kim, my twice publishing partner, thanks for making it possible for me to physically put this book into people's hands!

To all of the incredible people mentioned throughout this book, my coach Molly Carroll, Tony Robbins (one day I will meet you face-to-face!), my various mentors, especially Lou Diamond that helped me take my business to the next level, and my dear friends and family who were beyond patient as I explored my transformation. A special shout out to my dad who saved my ass more times than I want to admit—emotionally and financially.

Thank you for being the best Mr. Mom on the planet! To anyone who's name, or given title, is in this book, you were a part of my story and contributed to my getting where I am today. Thank you for your love, influence, and for being an important part of my journey.

And finally, thank you to all of my mom friends who are out there momming hard every day. Whether you have a full-time or part-time career that brings you an income, or your full-time career is being mom, you are nailing it with all you do and all you juggle! May we all be unapologetic on our quest for a juicy life.

Love,

Carrie

DANCING
MOON
PRESS